# ROYAL SCOTLAND

*Roddy Martine*

Paul Harris Publishing

Edinburgh & New York

First published 1983 by
Paul Harris Publishing
40 York Place
Edinburgh

ISBN 0 86228 045 1

Designed by Jenny Carter
Jacket design by James Hutcheson

Printed and bound in Great Britain
by Billings & Sons Limited, Worcester.

# Contents

# Introduction

IN a wonderfully pompous, at the same time historically acute pronouncement, Sir Walter Scott heralded King George IV's visit to Edinburgh in 1822.

"He is our kinsman," announced Sir Walter. "It is not too much to say that there is scarcely a gentleman of any of the old Scottish families who cannot 'count kin' with the Royal House from which our Sovereign is descended. In this small country blood has so intermingled that far the greater part of our burgesses and yeomen are entitled to entertain similar pretentions. In short, we are *the clan* and our King is *the Chief*. Let us remember that it is so, and not only look towards him as a father, but to teach each other as if we were, in the words of the old song, 'Ae man's bairns'".

There can be little doubt that this, or similar sentiment has formulated that magnificent arrogance so ingrained in the Scottish character. Sir Walter, ever a populist, was simply communicating what every Scot knows. And, indeed, it would explain the aggressive loyalty expressed by the people of Scotland towards successive Royal dynasties. Remember that Scotland's feudal tradition is uniquely different from that of England, embodied in the idea of Clanship and everything that remarkable concept encompassed. Although abandoned by King James VI for the South of England, the Highlands remained fiercely devoted to his Stuart descendants, even to the extent of rising in two rebellions on their behalf.

From 1650, when Charles II was crowned King of Scots at Scone, 172 years were to pass before a reigning British monarch was to set foot in Scotland. In 1852, Queen Victoria purchased

Balmoral Castle, 'this dear paradise', her Baronial mansion set in the rich forests of Deeside. Her enthusiasm for all things Scottish both before and after the death of Prince Albert, set the pattern of participation in Scottish life which has been enthusiastically followed by her descendants. The Royal Family's involvement in the traditional rituals of government and church is significant in that it embodies through pageantry the great passage of Scotland's history. Her Majesty the Queen's regular visits, both formal and informal, and her special love of life at Balmoral, remind us that the House of Windsor descends through the line of Stewart, their claim to the Throne of Scotland stretching far further back into the mists of antiquity than their claim to the Throne of England.

This book sets out to pay tribute to the Royal Houses of Scotland which through so many diverse routes descend into the current Royal House in Great Britain. Theirs is a rich, violent, colourful story, equal in drama to any of the great histories of the World.

# *Royal Scotland — from the merger of the Pictish and Celtic thrones to the death of the Maid of Norway*

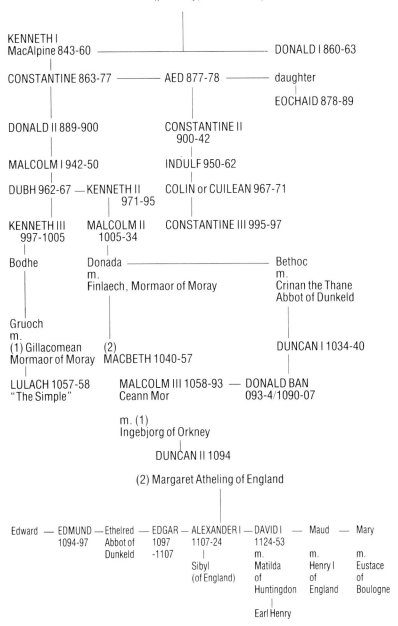

ALPIN 833-43 King of Dalriada
m. Heiress (probably) to Pictish Royal House

KENNETH I MacAlpine 843-60 ——————————— DONALD I 860-63

CONSTANTINE 863-77 ——— AED 877-78 ——— daughter

EOCHAID 878-89

DONALD II 889-900                CONSTANTINE II 900-42

MALCOLM I 942-50                INDULF 950-62

DUBH 962-67 — KENNETH II 971-95        COLIN or CUILEAN 967-71

KENNETH III 997-1005      MALCOLM II 1005-34      CONSTANTINE III 995-97

Bodhe        Donada ——————————— Bethoc
             m.                                    m.
             Finlaech, Mormaor of Moray            Crinan the Thane
                                                   Abbot of Dunkeld

Gruoch
m.
(1) Gillacomean      (2)                            DUNCAN I 1034-40
Mormaor of Moray    MACBETH 1040-57

LULACH 1057-58      MALCOLM III 1058-93 — DONALD BAN
"The Simple"        Ceann Mor              093-4/1090-07

m. (1)
Ingebjorg of Orkney

DUNCAN II 1094

(2) Margaret Atheling of England

Edward — EDMUND — Ethelred — EDGAR — ALEXANDER I — DAVID I — Maud — Mary
         1094-97   Abbot of   1097    1107-24       1124-53
         Dunkeld   -1107        |      m.           m.       m.       m.
                              Sibyl    Matilda      Henry I  Eustace
                              (of England)  of      of       of
                                         Huntingdon England  Boulogne

                                         Earl Henry

8

# 1

## The merger of the Thrones

ACROSS the tumbling stream of Laura in the district of Bere-gonium in Argyll stands the ancient Castle of Dunstaffnage. The present building dates from the 13th Century, but tradition has it that for centuries before then Dunstaffnage was the very centre of the Scots Kingdom of Dalriada until King Kenneth I MacAlpine moved his government to Scone in the ninth Century.

Others, however, acknowledge Dunadd, between Kilmartin and the Crinan Canal, as the rightful seat of the kings of Dalriada. There is a small hill, and near the summit, on a flat surface of rock, is the spot where the kings are said to have been crowned. A wild boar is carved in the rock, as is a footprint, said to be that of the witch of Cruachan. Another theory is that when kings were crowned, they would place the left foot in the footmark while being annointed with holy water. But there is little recorded information about Dunadd available although we know that it was attacked by Angus MacFergus, king of the Picts in the year 736. Perhaps it was after this that the kings of Dalriada chose to locate themselves at Dunstaffnage.

The succession of the Pictish throne tended to go to a male, but through female descent. During the early Christian period in Scotland, the Pictish kingdom had grown dramatically in power and expanded under King Angus MacFergus in the Eighth Century. Nobody knows quite where they came from, and indeed, the eventual disappearance on suffocation of their culture is equally veiled in mystery.

In the year 843, Alpin King of Scots died and was succeeded by his son Kenneth who claimed the throne of the Picts through his mother, a Pictish princess. One story goes that Kenneth arrived at Scone where he invited the Pictish king Drosten to a banquet; then, as his guests jovially consumed his food and wine, he had them slaughtered. This unsavoury example of hospitality could only be justified by the subsequent unification of the two kingdoms into what came to be known as Scotia.

It was to Dunstaffnage that the Lia-fail, the sacred stone of destiny on which the early kings of Ireland were crowned, had been brought by Fergus Mor Mac Erc, first king of Dalriada around the year 500. When Kenneth moved to Scone, the stone travelled with him.

Legend has it that the Lia-fail is the very stone on which Jacob rested his head the night he struggled with the Angel at Bethel. Via Egypt, it had been taken to Spain by Gathelus, progenitor of the Scottish/Irish peoples, and husband of Scota, daughter of Pharaoh Ramases II. From Spain the stone was transported to Ireland by Hiberus to throne the Irish Ard Righs.

For almost 800 years, all Scottish kings were crowned on this stone at Moot Hill, in front of Scone Palace. When Edward I of England invaded in 1296, he carried it off to England, although many believe that the Abbot of the day replaced the original with a lump of Scone sandstone. Certainly, geological evidence would tend to suggest this.

Whatever the truth, today the Stone of Destiny lies at Westminster beneath the throne of the United Kingdom, although still subject to the controversy which led to its theft by a group of Scottish Nationalists in the 1950s, and the outrage which accompanied this act underlines the deep significance which this unprepossessing rock holds in the hearts and minds of British Royalists.

Kenneth's removal to Scone was strategic, a policy followed by later monarchs who gradually manoeuvred their courts to the South as the realm expanded. To begin with, however, Perth was an ideal location from which to control the continually bickering and frequently warring tribal factions of North and South, at the same time seeking to check the constant threat of Viking invasion.

Originally, Vikings had come as raiders and pirates, but by Kenneth's time they had colonised Caithness, Orkney, Shetland and the Hebrides until this latter area became totally dominated by the Norsemen. Even York in England fell to their fierce and ruthless attacks. Conflict and regular skirmishes were part of life, and allegiances had to be continually reviewed. Kenneth's grandson King Constantine III found himself allied with Vikings and Welsh to counter an attack by Irish Vikings in 937. Defeat

*Scone Palace, on the outskirts of Perth. The present 19th Century castellated mansion is the seat of the Earl of Mansfield. Scottish kings were once traditionally crowned here at Moot Hill.*

followed through lack of liaison between the combined ranks, an inevitable conclusion one might say. Despite this, however, by 971, Strathclyde (Cumbria) and Lothian with its old Brython fortress of Dun Eideann (Edinburgh) had come into the kingdom of Scotland, and in 1018, a victory at Carham wiped out the Northumbrian kingdom bringing Scotland's boundaries to the River Tweed.

When Malcolm II died in 1034, he had more or less established the realm of Scotland as it exists today, although Thorfinn II, one of Malcolm's grandsons through a convenient marriage between his daughter and the Norse Jarl Sigurd the Strut, ruled the islands from Shetland to Dublin owing allegiance only to King Magnus Barefoot of Norway.

Malcolm II's death left the House of Alpin without a male-heir, and consequently, by his expressed wish, the throne passed to his eldest grandson whom he had already established as King of Strathclyde. Malcolm's eldest daughter Bethoc had married Crinan the Thane, Lay Abbot of Dunkeld, a kinsman of St Columba no less, and their son became the new King Duncan I. This succession finally united the kingdoms of Scotia, Lothian and Strathclyde, but there were those for whom this achievement signified little.

Another of Malcolm's daughters had married Finlaech, Mormaer of Moray and their son was MacBeth, who, through marriage to the Lady Gruoch, a grand-daughter of King Kenneth III, considered his claim to the throne to be considerably more valid than that of his cousin. In this belief he was supported by Thorfinn, since King Duncan had unwisely demanded tribute from Thorfinn's Earldom of Caithness.

William Shakespeare's brilliant and sensitive tragedy, based on the notes of the 16th Century English chronicler Raphael Holinshed, does much injustice to MacBeth, the more violent initiative in the plot being perpetrated by Thorfinn, at least to begin with. It should also be appreciated that Shakespeare's play is heavily weighted in favour of Banquo's line from which had descended the Stewart dynasty represented by Shakespeare's monarch and patron King James VI and I. Banquo, most probably never existed, but materialised as an invention to give the Stewarts a credible Scottish lineage.

In desperation, Duncan appointed his nephew Mumtan to be Earl of Caithness to supercede Thorfinn in 1040. He was despatched North with an army which was soundly defeated in Sutherland. Duncan's fleet which had been sent off as back-up support was summarily scattered off Durness, and the unfortunate Mumtan was burned to death in his headquarters at Thurso. Meanwhile, MacBeth had decided to make his claim public, and Duncan, with yet another army marched to make battle at Torfness where he was killed on the battlefield.

MacBeth now ascended the throne and, indeed, ruled relatively successfully for 17 years. Duncan's Queen had been a relative of the Danish Earl Siward who governed Northern England under King Edward the Confessor. It was to York, therefore, that Duncan's elder son Malcolm was sent for safety, while the younger, Donald Ban, took refuge in the Western Isles. Their separation, as we shall see, was to be significant in years to come.

MacBeth, meanwhile, completed his carnage against the House of Dunkeld by killing Crinan in 1045, while Thorfinn the Mighty returned peaceably to Caithness where he married a young Norwegian princess called Ingibjorg. At a later date, he and MacBeth made a journey through Norway, Denmark and Germany, to Rome, where this violent couple were absolved of their sins by the Pope.

The well-known historical novelist, Dorothy Dunnett, researching in Norway and Denmark, has come up with the suggestion that Thorfinn and MacBeth were one and the same person. It *is* possible that "Thorfinn" being a "heathen" name acceptable for a ruler of Orkney, was not considered a suitable "christian" appellation for a King of Alba. The same might be said concerning "Ingibjorg" and "Gruoch". From what we know, the lives of the two men ran surprisingly parallel and the documentation is so slight that there are many anomalies. So it could be that Ms Dunnett's theory is correct, thereby radically changing what has come to be accepted, but for the purposes of this narrative, until further evidence emerges, we can only speculate and follow the traditional history.

What we do know is that MacBeth, as a monarch, proved to be both wise and popular. Scotland settled down to a period of relative prosperity enhanced by the flowering influence of the Celtic church. But, naturally, it could not last.

As the years passed, the exiled Malcolm grew to maturity. With his kinsman, Siward, he plotted and planned his revenge, and by 1054, he was ready to invade. On the first occasion he succeeded in conquering Lothian and Cumbria, and three years later he met and killed MacBeth at Lumphanan in Aberdeenshire.

Immediately, Lulach, Lady Gruoch's son by a previous marriage, and undoubtedly prompted by his ambitious mother, claimed the throne. Lulach was known as "the Simple", and the name was apt if he believed that he could keep his crown from Malcolm. Within months he had been despatched to join his step-father.

King Malcolm III Ceann Mor (Big Head) was to rule for 35 years. Although reputed to have few graces and an inability to read or write, his reign was to mark a watershed in Scotland's development. At the same time, Anglo-Saxon rule in England was crushed by the invasion of Duke William of Normandy in 1066.

*The House of Dunkeld*
Some historians suggest that Malcolm first married his cousin Ingibjorg, Thorfinn's widow. It seems unlikely that the same Ingibjorg would have relished such a match with the murderer of her husband's friend or, indeed, that Malcolm would have wished wedlock with the wife of his father's triumphant enemy. But remember that these were violent times, death and conflict everyday encounters and life expectancy short. Alliances were forged out of convenience, usually for the acquisition of power or for protection. And often as not, throughout history, the bloodiest confrontations were affected between the closest of kin. Besides, Ingibjorg was said to be very beautiful. A more likely theory is that the Ingibjorg in question could have been Thorfinn's daughter, particularly as there is some discrepancy regarding dates, but certainly it was through her control of the Castle of Dingwall that Malcolm was able to exercise considerable sway over his northern territories. They had three children, the eldest of whom was later to reign as King Duncan II. Quite what happened to the Queen eventually is anybody's guess — records do not tell us. Possibly it was on the grounds of consanguinity that Malcolm managed to arrange a divorce, for in 1069 he took for his second wife the Saxon Princess Margaret Atheling, a refugee from the Norman conquest.

It seems an unlikely match. Margaret of England may have been a great beauty; she was certainly strong-willed, devout and educated, and was so much loved during her lifetime that less than 200 years after her death she was canonized.

Her arrival at Malcolm's Capital of Dunfermline was via the Binks rocks at what is now known as Queensferry. From here she was ferried across the Firth of Forth, and at a later date Malcolm granted permanent free crossing of the Firth for pilgrims in passage to St Andrews. The crossing therefore became known as Passagium Reginae — the Queen's Passage or Ferry.

*St Columba landed on the west coast Island of Iona in 563. Scottish kings were brought here for burial until the 11th Century.*

To Dunfermline she brought the culture and ceremonial style of her Hungarian Anglicised background, but she was not over-enamoured of the "fort of the crooked line" where Malcolm had chosen to live. Their tower was built on a mound and surrounded on three sides by the glen. A fragment of this castle still exists in Pittencrieffe Park, a little west of the later palace.

Nevertheless, in 1075 Margaret founded a Benedictine Priory here, which was later raised to the rank of an Abbey by her son David, the youngest of the seven children she bore Malcolm. Most of what we know of Queen Margaret comes from her confessor Turgot's Life of the Queen. And from this source we learn that Malcolm, the tyrant, was totally infatuated, supporting her every desire and being guided single-mindedly by her council. It was under such influence therefore that a form of feudalism was introduced to Scottish government, thereby bringing Scotland in line with the rest of Europe. And it was Margaret who set out to import the influences of the Church of Rome, ironing out the irregularities inherent in the Celtic Church. The consequence was that Scotland became more European in its outlook and less insular, a development much resented by upholders of the old order.

Meantime Duke William had established himself in England with some considerable flair. Aware both that his main challenger, Margaret's brother Edgar the Atheling was being sheltered in Scotland, and that Malcolm had initiated forays over the Border, he marched North with a powerful army, the like of which the Scots had never seen. Malcolm, being no fool, realised he could not possibly challenge such a force, and acquiesced, receiving William peacably at Abernethy, where he took an oath of allegiance. This submission was the first of many to cause complications between the two countries for centuries to follow. It did not help either that William demanded that Malcolm's eldest son Duncan be sent to the English Court as a pledge of peace.

Peace, however, lasted only seven years and in 1079, Malcolm invaded Northumbria. King William Rufus summoned him to his Court at Gloucester in 1092 and Malcolm accepted. On his way, he called at Durham and was present at the foundation of Durham Cathedral. On reaching Gloucester, however, William refused to see him unless he did homage for his kingdom. Outraged, Malcolm refused, and on his homeward journey was ambushed and killed at a place afterwards called Malcolm's Cross, near Alnwick in 1093.

Margaret, it is said, foresaw this event. Some say she was forewarned by a Highland seer. Whatever the case, she had come to pass her days almost exclusively in devotional practices, even to the extent of becoming ill in the process.

She had turned to the ancient castle of Dun Eideann on its rock, and had established a palace here. It was at Edinburgh then that she received the news of her husband's death, and also that of their eldest son, Edward. Resigning herself to the will of God, it is said she died with the same saintly humility which had made her so beloved by her people. The Chapel which stands to this day at Edinburgh Castle, the one building there to be left standing after its capture by Sir Thomas Ranulph, Earl of Moray in 1313, was dedicated to her memory by King David I.

Now Malcolm Cean Mor had ruled Scotland with an iron fist. For 35 years he had mastered his realm with a determination, efficiency and success unmatched by his predecessors. But ghosts are apt to rise in times of great confusion and little had been heard of his younger brother Donald Ban's doings in the Western Isles.

Known as "The Fair" or "The White", one can assume he had blonde hair, although at the time of his re-emergence it had presumably become white. Donald Ban was well into his sixties when he attacked his nephews at Edinburgh Castle, catching them completely off their guard and still reeling from the loss of both father, mother and brother. By cover of night, however, they managed to escape taking with them their mother's body to Dunfermline, where she was interred. From there, they fled to William in England where they found that their hostage half-brother Duncan had become one of the King's favourites.

The King of England affected horror at Donald Ban's action, indeed appeared full of remorse at Malcolm's slaying, even to the extent of confining the Earl of Northumbria to perpetual imprisonment. Under the Celtic laws of Tanistry, however, the Mormaors of Scotland accepted Donald as their monarch. It was a different situation when six months later Duncan marched on Scotland with an Anglo-Norman army, and claimed his throne by hereditary right, not conquest. His Charter was witnessed by his eldest half-brother Edgar, which emphasises that Margaret's sons approved. All that is save Edmund.

Duncan's first mistake was no doubt to show leniency towards his wild uncle. Whether or not he was directly involved in what was to follow will never be known, but when Edmund made intimations towards his exiled uncle, Duncan was surprised and murdered by the Mormaor of the Mearns at Mondynes in Kincardineshire.

Uncle and Nephew immediately seized the throne becoming joint-sovereigns. Donald Ban ruled north of the Forth and Clyde; Edmund, South to the Border. They could not seriously have expected to hold out for long, and within three years Edgar and the brothers were back. Donald Ban did not get off so lightly this time for Edgar had his eyes put out and he was imprisoned for the remainder of his life. Edmund, his life spared, was allowed to become a monk.

The fundamental problem inherited by Queen Margaret's sons was the widespread resentment felt towards the changes she had brought about — changes at Court, changes in the Church, above all, changes in the system by which Scotland was governed. The sudden upsurge of support for Donald Ban, if short lived, can be attributed to his rough treatment of the many anglo-saxon settlers, many of whom were either executed or sent back from whence they came.

But Queen Margaret's sons continued her work, and it was Edgar who finally moved the Capital to Edinburgh, although not fully appreciating that he was taking his centre of administration significantly further away from his Highland subjects and from the lands of his ancestors. It was at this stage in Scotland's history that pockets of local government began to form in the lawless Highlands, factions which emerged as the Clan system. Edgar's 10 years on Scotland's throne thereafter were not eventful. He was known as "the Peaceable", possibly a result of his rather meekly ceding the Western Isles to Magnus Barelegs, King of Norway in 1098.

Edgar's brother, King Alexander I, succeeded in 1107, and perhaps the most interesting fact about him is that he had married Sibyl, the natural daughter of King Henry I of England. The two kingdoms had become even more closely allied when King Henry married Alexander's sister, the Princess Matilda of Scotland, England's Good Queen Maud, so one sees that the links between the two thrones were remarkably incestuous.

Alexander I ruled Scotland for 17 years and earned the name of Alexander the Fierce for his merciless treatment of a rebellion in Moray. He was deeply religious and a strong king, but like his elder brothers, he died childless. It was his younger brother King David I, 41 years old when he ascended the throne, who truely guided his country out of the dark ages, and he is remembered as the most significant of the sons of Queen Margaret and King Malcom Ceann Mor.

*Honouring an age old tradition, Her Majesty the Queen attended a ceremony at the High Kirk of St Giles accompanied by her Hereditary Officers of State on the occasion of her Silver Jubilee Celebrations in 1977.*

# From 1124 to the death of King Alexander III, 1286

DAVID I
1124-53
m.
Matilda
of Huntingdon
|
Earl Henry
|

MALCOLM IV 1153-65 ——— WILLIAM 1165-1214 ——— David
(The Maiden)                  (The Lion)                          Earl of Huntingdon

m.
Ermengarde
de
Beaumont
|
ALEXANDER II
1214-49

m.
(1)
Joan of
England

(2)
Mary de
Coucy
|
ALEXANDER III
1249-86

m.
(1)
Margaret of England

(2)
Yolande de
Dreaux
|

Alexander ——— David ——— Margaret

m.
Erik II
of Norway
|
MARGARET 1286-90
(The Maid of Norway)

# 2

## Scotland's Golden Age

EARL David had spent his early years at the English Court and during his brother's reign had ruled Cumbria and part of Lothian. Most significantly, however, he had married Matilda of Huntingdon, widow of the Earl of Northampton, grand-niece of William the Conqueror and grand-daughter of Earl Siward, from whom she had inherited great wealth, a claim to his earldom of Northumbria and the territories of Huntingdon. Earl David therefore became one of the greatest vassals of the English monarchy.

The Feudal System meant simply that those who worked the land could do so in return for military service to their feudal superior, who, in turn held such lands in return for supporting the monarch. Where this system differed from the Clan concept was that the latter was essentially a family society comprising all the ramifications of duty, loyalty and pride. It is notable that such sentiments were rarely evident between serf and vassal.

A problem then inevitably arose when a Scottish king who held lands in England was called upon to do homage to the king of England, who not surprisingly maintained that because the king of Scots was his vassal, then Scotland itself must be subject to his dictate.

When David, Earl of Huntingdon, came to the throne of Scotland in 1124, he brought many of his Anglo-Norman friends with him — Robert de Brus, Hugo de Moreville and Walter FitzAlan included. The latter was installed as Royal Steward, an office from which his family was to acquire the name of Stewart. These friends were established in the south of Scotland as powerful feudal barons. In consequence, many of the more established lords removed themselves to the West or North. While relations between Scotland and its powerful neighbour remained relatively amiable, David was able to build up an efficient system of government, recording feudal dues in charters and setting up a staff of royal officers whose rule was to run the kingdom. A royal council was established consisting of the king's relatives, his noblemen and representatives of the church.

Queen Margaret's devotion had made a profound impression on her children, and not least, on David. It became his policy to build great Abbeys, and in doing so, introduce points of civilisation to hitherto deprived areas of his realm. These were perhaps his most enduring contribution. Before coming to the throne, he had established the See of Glasgow as earl of Strathclyde, and before his death, the bishoprics of Moray, Dunkeld, Galloway, Caithness, Ross, Aberdeen, Brechin and Dunblane.

There did, however, ensue a feud with England over a decision by the Pope not to appoint a Scottish Archbishop insisting that Scottish bishops be subordinate to the Archbishop of York. And when Henry I died and Civil War broke out in England between Henry's daughter Matilda and her cousin Stephen, who usurped the throne, the matter took on a certain political significance.

David was uncle to Matilda and to Stephen's wife, also called Matilda, but he had sworn fealty to the former and therefore rallied to her cause with certain conditions. Stephen marched north with a great army, whereupon David was forced to make peace. In 1138, however, he invaded England on Matilda's behalf, but after a crushing defeat at Cutton Moor, known as the Battle of the Standard, he retreated to Carlisle. In 1141, he was at Matilda's side again, accompanying her from London to Winchester. This time he was nearly captured and decided thereafter to remain in Scotland.

The powerful Gothic or romanesque architecture of the 12th Century monastic buildings reminds us that this was a time when Scotland shone in the light of European enlightenment. Cisterian monasteries were founded at Melrose, Newbattle, Dundrennan and Kinloss; Tironesian at Selkirk, Kelso and Arbroath. The Benedictine church at Dunfermline was constructed over St Margaret's church and dedicated in 1150, and David also continued his brother Alexander's patronage of the

*A winter view of the remains of Melrose Abbey, founded for Cistercian monks in the 12th Century.*

22

Augustinian movement founding abbeys at Holyrood, Jedburgh and Stirling. All this was done partly, of course, with a view to pleasing the Vatican, whose enormous financial and political power dominated all nations' foreign policies. Towards the end of the Century, indeed, the Pope relented in his policy towards Scotland. The Scottish church owed its obedience directly to the Pope and not via an English Archbishop. Henceforth Scottish kings could carry the golden papal rose as part of their regalia.

When David died at Carlisle in 1153, he left behind a well-organised country with prospering towns growing under his royal protection. These centres of trade and industry had evolved from little villages and taken on a significant identity in the economic structure of a new concept of society. Land was still the economic basis of a country's prosperity, but with the towns came commerce, and in general the standard of living for the poor in Scotland was far ahead of that in England or France. David's death, unfortunately, left Scotland in turmoil. His son Henry had predeceased him and his grandson Malcolm succeeded at the age of eleven. Known as "the Maiden", Malcolm IV resigned his grandfather's claims to the north of England and paid homage to Henry II of England for Huntingdon. Scotland began to fall apart again. In the North and West, the king of Norway and Somerled, legendary ancestor of Clan Donald, wrought havoc. Without a strong ruler, Scottish lords became divided in their loyalties. It is usually said that Malcolm IV acquired his nickname from an effeminate appearance, hardly surprising when one considers his extreme youth. Equally, however, it could have had something to do with a vow of chastity, for he never married, and he was universally respected as an exceptionally holy youth, compared by some with Thomas Becket. He was to die at the age of 23 having ruled for 12 years and, all considered, should not be dismissed as unsuccessful. Faced with rebellions in Galloway, Argyll and Moray, Malcolm IV and his administration wasted little time in suppressing them, thus clearing the way for his 22-year old brother to turn his attention to regaining their father's English conquests.

The opportunity came after the murder of Thomas Becket. William "the Lion" invaded England and besieged Carlisle while Henry II was facing his own sons' rebellion. To begin with the invasion went well with victories in Cumberland and Westmorland, but then William was captured at Alnwick. Henry, a strong minded and violent tempered individual, imprisoned his cousin in Normandy and in 1174 forced him to acknowledge him as over-lord of Scotland in return for his freedom.

Humiliated, William was allowed to return to Scotland in 1175 and, surprisingly, Scotland prospered. William had been a friend of Becket, but one can assume that this was not entirely his reason for dedicating his Abbey of Arbroath to the newly canonised saint in 1178. Ways of embarrassing the English king were not that easily found. In 1189, Henry II of England died, and his heir, Richard Coeur de Lion set about realising his dream of a Crusade to the Holy Land. He needed money and William offered 10,000 merks in return for the restoration of his sovereign rights. Astonishingly, Richard agreed.

The 'Quitclaim of Canterbury' utterly vindicated Scotland from English claims of Over-lordship; the terms and wording entirely clear. In years to come this agreement was continually referred to by Scotland and repeatedly dismissed by England, but for the time being Scotland was universally recognised as its own. William had literally bought back his inheritance.

It is believed that at this time Scotland adopted the Lion Rampant as the Royal Arms, and, indeed, this could be the reason that William acquired his nickname. His strong "lion-like" physical appearance is attributed as another reason, and he was revered as a "Lion of Justice". But this was an age of lions, and Scotland's William was no exception.

Although it is known that he fathered several children, William did not marry until he was 44. His Queen, Ermengarde de Beaumont bore him three daughters and one son, but the latter was not conceived until 1198. But William the Lion lived to be 72, a great age for those days. Latterly he faced rebellions from grandsons of Duncan II, but these were speedily quelled and when he died, he had the satisfaction of knowing that he had restored his kingdom to prosperity and that his son was well able to continue the work.

Many regard the 13th Century in Scotland as a golden age. Much was achieved, not least in exterior relations. William the Lion's two eldest daughters had been sent to the English court to be married to sons of King John. A 15,000 merk dowry accompanied them, but the English king failed to comply with the bargain. It was no surprise when Alexander II supported the Magna Carta of 1215.

It was important, however, that a good relationship be established between the two kingdoms, and Alexander later agreed to marry Princess Joan, King John's daughter and sister to the new King Henry III. All was not yet resolved for Alexander still resented the loss of his sisters' dowry. He bided his time until an opportune moment presented itself — Henry was facing a Baronial revolt — and then demanded its return along with the lands Malcolm had ceded to Henry II. In 1236, the brothers-in-law met at York and in 1237 officially agreed the Tweed-Solway line as marking the Border. Alexander abandoned his claim for the northern English counties, receiving Tynedale and Penrith for an annual rental of one red falcon. The dowry was never returned, but the Scottish Princesses married English nobility and everybody seemed to be happy with the arrangement. Queen Joan, alas, died childless in 1238, and anxious to beget an heir, Alexander hastily married Marie, daughter of a wealthy French baron, Enguerrand de Coucy. At last, in 1241, a son was born.

With improved agricultural methods, trade prospered and

*Fortrose Abbey on the Black Isle, founded by King David I for the See of Ross. It is said that Cromwell used many of the Cathedral's stones to build a fort at Inverness.*

townships grew. Money increasingly replaced produce as currency and fine building in the Gothic style took place, notably Glasgow Cathedral, which can be admired to this day.

As has already been noted, Alexander II was a man of peace, although not averse to a show of strength. Diplomacy, became increasingly a key to his policies.

The French marriage proved unpopular with England who as ever regarded France as their major adversary. Feelings on either side of the Border became tense again. By way of appeasement, therefore, a betrothal was arranged between Alexander's eldest son and Henry III's daughter, Princess Margaret. Conflict from another quarter, however, was always prevalent, and Alexander determined that the question should be settled once and for all. Disturbances had continually taken place on the West Coast and in the Far North. The need to control the Western Isles became increasingly apparent to the king, and yet these had been controlled for generations by the kings of Norway. Alexander set about negotiations, but having failed, force seemed the only path open. Then, unexpectedly, while on the Islet of Kerrera, off Oban, he died. His son and heir was seven years old.

In 1251, the boy-king Alexander III of Scotland was married to Princess Margaret of England. Both nations rejoiced. Alexander was knighted by his father-in-law and did homage for his English lands. Inevitably he was invited to do homage for Scotland, but shrewdly and politely declined. The point was made, yet 21 years later, at the Coronation of King Edward I of England, the matter was raised and disregarded again. Edward and Alexander respected one another; as brothers-in-law they settled to ruling their respective kingdoms in harmony.

On acquiring his majority, Alexander had determined to fulfill his father's purpose regarding the Western Isles. Once again negotiations were opened and failed. Force was inevitable, and in 1263 King Haakon of Norway set sail for Scotland with a force comprising 160 Longships and an army numbering up to 20,000. Alexander, meanwhile, had filled his castle in the West with armed men and his main force was waiting on Camphill, between Kilbirnie and Largs.

On 1st October 1263, a gale blew up driving a detatchment of the Norwegian fleet ashore. The Viking invaders were fiercely repulsed by the waiting Scots and their store-ship stranded (in the Scottish National Portrait Gallery is a fresco depicting this victory). Both sides, however, claimed victory, but the fact is that King Haakon, well advanced in his years, fell back to Kirkwall, on Orkney, to recuperate, and in December, he died.

Diplomacy followed and in 1266, King Magnus IV of Norway ceded the Hebrides and Man to Scotland in return for a payment of 4,000 merks in four annual instalments and 100 merks in perpetuity.

Although the Battle of Largs brought Alexander immense popularity and aided him greatly in establishing law and order in the remoter corners of his realm, personal loss was to colour his life. Queen Joan, by contemporary account, a woman of "great beauty, chastity and humility", died in 1275. One son died in infancy, while the second, Alexander, died at the age of 20. This left only a daughter, Margaret, who had been married to Eric II of Norway in 1281 as a pledge of peace. The King of Scotland's grand-daughter now emerged as heir to the Scots throne.

In 1285, Alexander married again; this time to Yolande (or Joleta), daughter of Robert IV, Count of Dreux. She was the "fairest of women" and their marriage took place at Jedburgh Abbey. While the congregation danced and sang at the wedding feast, the appearance of a shadowy phantom-like apparition fore-warned a superstitious Scotland of the tragedy to come.

The king, it was said, was passionately in love with his new bride. He could scarce bear to be parted from her company and this was, indeed, to be the cause of his end. He had been attending a Council at Edinburgh Castle and the Queen awaited him across the Firth of Forth at the royal residence of Pettycur, near Kinghorn. In the best MacBeth tradition it was a wild and stormy night, but the king could not be dissuaded from making the crossing. His companions gave prayers of thanks for their safe delivery to the other shore where horses were provided, but in the darkness the King was separated from them. On a cliff, only a short passage from his destination, the King's horse stumbled and Alexander fell to his death on the rocks below. That fatal night was to precipitate turmoil in Scotland. With Alexander's death, wrote the chronicler Andrew of Wyntoun, "Oure gold was chengit to lede".

# From the accession of the little Maid of Norway to the Coronation at Scone of King Robert I

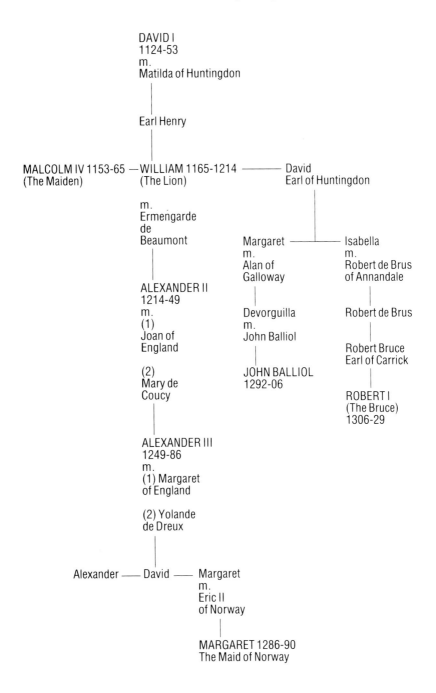

DAVID I
1124-53
m.
Matilda of Huntingdon

Earl Henry

MALCOLM IV 1153-65 — WILLIAM 1165-1214 ———— David
(The Maiden)            (The Lion)                        Earl of Huntingdon

m.
Ermengarde
de
Beaumont                        Margaret ———— Isabella
                                m.                 m.
                                Alan of            Robert de Brus
                                Galloway           of Annandale

ALEXANDER II
1214-49
m.                              Devorguilla        Robert de Brus
(1)                             m.
Joan of                         John Balliol
England                                            Robert Bruce
                                                   Earl of Carrick
(2)                             JOHN BALLIOL
Mary de                         1292-06
Coucy                                              ROBERT I
                                                   (The Bruce)
                                                   1306-29

ALEXANDER III
1249-86
m.
(1) Margaret
of England

(2) Yolande
de Dreux

Alexander —— David —— Margaret
                      m.
                      Eric II
                      of Norway

                      MARGARET 1286-90
                      The Maid of Norway

# 3

# The Road to Turmoil

MARGARET, Maid of Norway, was three years of age when her grandfather fell to his death on the bleak Fife shore. Such had been the way with marriages of state that the young Erik II of Norway was barely 14 when he fathered his child in 1283, his Scottish bride some seven years older. The little Princess, however, through primogeniture was recognised immediately as the heiress to the throne of Scotland and a government consisting of six Guardians of the Realm was appointed during her minority.

Ever present, needless to say, was the shadow of her great-uncle, the English king. It made sense, insisted Edward I. Margaret should marry his eldest son, Prince Edward of England. Through this splendid match they would one day rule England and Scotland independently, but also, God willing, their heir could unite the two kingdoms. One can only conjecture on the passage of history had this situation come about.

In 1289, the Treaty of Salisbury and in 1290, the Treaty of Birgham, confirmed that the marriage should take place. The Guardians — the Bishops of St Andrews and Glasgow, the Earls of Fife and Buchan, the Lord of Badenoch and the Steward — nevertheless asserted that the "rights, laws, liberties and customs of Scotland" should not be violated.

The story is full of pathos. Delighted with the marriage agreement, the King of England proposed a fine ship to bring the little Queen to her country. Her father, however, had other ideas. She was, after all, a Princess of the Norwegian Royal House. So in 1290 she set sail on a Norwegian ship accompanied by Bishop Narve of Bergen. King Edward's commissioners awaited her arrival at Skelbo Castle, near Dornoch on the Scottish mainland, and it was here that they received the news that the seven year old Queen had died on the crossing. The stricken ship sailed into the Orkney bay off South Ronaldsay, near Kirkwall, and then the body was returned to Bergen.

As is inevitable with such tragedies, there has been a deal of speculation surrounding what exactly did happen, but there is no particular reason to suppose that the little girl removed from home and father, on a rough sea voyage, should not have become mortally sick. Nor is it particularly strange that King Erik should have required the coffin to be opened on its return so that he should identify the body. The bizarre sequel was that, some years later, after King Erik's death, a young woman from Liebeck in Germany came forward claiming to be Queen Margaret. A public trial and denouncement followed, and the luckless lady, whoever she was, was burned as a witch.

Meanwhile, what of Scotland? A complicated tangle of intermarriage and precedence was central to the inheritance of the Scottish throne. As we have seen, when David I ascended many of his friends accompanied him to Scotland. It was not surprising therefore that their children inter-married. Besides, from the days before the Norman conquest these great families were already related; Flemings who had married Flemings, descendants of Charlemagne. Thwarted in his ambitions to unite and control the two kingdoms, Edward of England asserted himself as over-Lord. There were thirteen claimants to the Scottish throne, and it became only politic that William Fraser, bishop of St Andrews and the magnates of Scotland should turn to Edward to help decide the issue.

At Norham in May 1291, twenty-four English and eighty Scots nobles and the English king met to decide the matter. Now Malcolm the Maiden and William the Lion had had a younger brother, David, Earl of Huntingdon, and this was the most direct line of succession from King David I. Earl David had had three daughters — Margaret, Isabella and Ada, and it was therefore their descendants who were considered to be the most serious contenders. Margaret had married Alan, Lord of Galloway and their daughter Devorguilla was therefore a great heiress, reputed to possess 30 Knight's fees in England and to own half the lands of Galloway. Devorguilla married John Balliol from the powerful Norman family who had come to England with the

*Sweetheart Abbey, founded for Cistercian monks by Devorguilla, mother of King John Balliol.*

Conquest. Founded by Guido de Balliol who held the fiefs of Bailleul, Pampierre, Harcourt and Vinoy in Normandy, they received lands in the North of England from King William II of England and built Barnard Castle at Durham. John Balliol had acted as Regent during the minority of Alexander III, but being accused of treason had fled South and appeared fighting for King Henry III of England against Simon de Montfort. He founded several scholarships at Oxford and after his death Devorguilla established the college which bears his name.

Devorguilla was a devoutly religious lady and founded many priories. Theirs had been a marriage of love and after his death, she carried her husband's heart with her at all times until her own death some sixteen years later. In Dumfriesshire she founded Sweetheart Abbey for Cisterian monks from Dundrennan, and it is here that she and her husband are buried. Tragically, her tomb was desecrated, but a reconstruction was made in the south transept and a memorial slab marks the original site. John and Devorguilla had four sons, one of whom, also John was considered most eligible as heir to Scotland's throne.

Earl David's second daughter, however, had married Robert de Brus, Lord of Annandale. Their son, also Robert de Brus, naturally contested the claim on the basis that he was a grandson of King David I whereas Balliol was a great-grandson, and secondly, before the birth of King Alexander III, he, Robert de Brus had been recognised by King Alexander II as next heir.

As adjudicator, King Edward I of England demanded that all claimants should recognise him as feudal superior. None wished their chances to be prejudiced, so they naturally complied. Besides, Balliol and Bruce through their English lands were already his vassals. After deep and considered study, King Edward announced that he had decided in favour of the nearest heir by primogeniture, John Balliol. Apart from his choice being unquestionably the right one, Edward was probably aware that Balliol was the best candidate from his personal requirements. The King of England was determined to dominate Scotland in the way he had succeeded in doing in Wales. On announcing Balliol's nomination, Edward demanded that he should repeat his oath of allegiance. Balliol had little choice. Scotland was already divided, many feeling that Bruce should have been successful. Balliol, therefore, needed Edward's support.

It is easy to criticise Balliol. At the time, however, it would have been virtually impossible to find any successful middle course between Edward Plantagenet's obsession to impose his will on Scotland and the deliberately provocative and powerful faction supporting Bruce and others. Balliol, nevertheless, made a fundamental error when he later confiscated Bruce lands and gave them to his cousins, the powerful Comyn family.

On St Andrew's Day 1292, John Balliol was crowned King of Scots at Scone. On 26th December he did homage for Scotland at Newcastle. Edward's designs seemed to have been fully met and he returned to his old feud with King Philip IV of France. The English king continued nevertheless to treat his Scottish cousin with contempt at every opportunity; for his part, Balliol was in the position of continually having to assert his position as king, even to his own subjects many of whom would not forgive him for accepting Edward's terms. A particular example came to a head when a Scottish vassal carried his case to Edward, who no doubt found it amusing to summon Balliol to England to answer the claims against him. Balliol complied and in May 1294 attended a parliament in London. Not long afterwards Edward summoned him to do military service in France; it seemed that the English king would miss no opportunity to humiliate the King of Scots.

This time, however, Balliol decided to take a stand. He appointed a Council of Twelve and in 1295 he signed a Treaty of Allegiance with France. Englishmen were dismissed from the court, and this was the first of many treaties in generations to come binding Scotland and France together in friendship in what was to become known as the Auld Alliance. King Edward was understandably outraged. From this moment the English king took off the mantel of "The Hammer of the Scots". He attacked Berwick, then Scotland's richest port, and massacred the inhabitants. At Dunbar, faced with little resistance, he won a second, decisive victory. One should note that among Edward's followers at this stage was the young Robert Bruce, Earl of Carrick.

In July 1296, Balliol surrendered his kingdom at Brechin to Antony Tek, bishop of Durham as representative of the English king. Shortly afterwards, he appeared before Edward at Montrose handing him a white rod, the feudal token of resignation. With his son, also Edward, Balliol was taken to the Tower of London in chains and there he remained for 3 years before being exiled to France at the request of Pope Boniface VIII. It was a crushing disaster for the Balliol family, and seemingly, for Scotland. All the old rivalries flamed up again, but above all escalated the resistance to any English king holding sway. John Balliol, meantime, was to pass his remaining years quietly on his estates in France with, not surprisingly, no desire to return to his former kingdom. He died in Normandy in 1315 having no doubt heard of the great Scots victory

*The remains of Lochmaben Castle, Dumfries. For years, this was the headquarters of the Bruce family, and there is some evidence to suggest that King Robert I was born here.*

at Bannockburn. He left several children by his wife Isabel, daughter of John de Warenne, Earl of Surrey, but it was not until after 1324 that the Balliols were again considered in regard to the Scottish throne.

Watching as Balliol was stripped of his royal insignia and armorial bearings at Brechin was the young Robert Bruce. One wonders how he felt when it was announced that the Stone of Destiny, so dear to the hearts of Scottish republicans, was to be removed south to Westminster. Was it then that his destiny began to make itself clear?

Bruce was 22 years old and had spent his youth at the English court. His birthplace, however, is believed to have been in Scotland, either at the Bruce stronghold of Lochmaben in Dumfriesshire, or more likely, at Turnberry, his mother's castle of the Ayrshire coast. Be that as it may, he would obviously have been deeply involved in the suit for the the crown of Scotland, and, indeed, it was Balliol's success which prompted his grandfather to resign Annandale to his son, the 7th Robert, who later assumed the title Lord of Annandale. By 1292 this Robert had already made over the earldom of Carrick to his son who presented the deed of resignation to Balliol at Stirling in 1293, offering the homage which his father and grandfather were unwilling to render. Feudal custom required that the king should take seisin of the earldom before re-granting it and receiving homage, and the sheriff of Ayr was directed to take it on the king's behalf. It was at this time that the disputes between Balliol and Edward escalated and although it is a moot point, it is unlikely that Bruce did render homage.

The young Bruce seems to have had a close relationship with the English king. In 1294 he was granted permission to visit Ireland for a year and a half, and Edward also allowed him respite of all the debts owed by him to the Exchequer. Being large landowners in England with many manors, chiefly in Yorkshire, both Bruces, father and son, sided with Edward against Balliol.

In times of national crisis a hero invariably arises sooner or later — a person, possibly unknown until some event precipitates them to take up the mantel of leadership. Such a man was William Wallace of Elderslie, son of a humble Ayrshire squire. Both rough and tough, Wallace emerged as a ruthless, determined fighter dedicated to freeing his country from exploitation. They say his obsessive hatred of the English sprang from the murder of his wife, Mary Braidfute by English troops at Lanark. Revenge on Haselrigg, the Governor of Lanark Castle and Sheriff of Ayr, whom he stabbed to death, did not suffice. While the young Robert Bruce deliberated on his future allegiances, Scotland had found a general.

History understandable romanticises its heroes; to many of that day, particularly the English, Wallace must have appeared as a contemporary Che Guevera, a dangerous outlaw with a certain amount of passionate appeal. But Edward's policies of subjugation rallied a people who were simply not prepared to be downtrodden. Led by James Stewart and Bishop Wishart, a major national resistance movement was being mobilised. In the North, Andrew de Moray and his uncle, the Bishop of Moray, were similarly employed. Meanwhile, in 1297, William Wallace burned the Barns of Ayr, the temporary barracks erected by Edward, and with them their 500 occupants — an appalling act of savagery.

Not long after, at Stirling Bridge, an English army was totally smashed by Wallace's forces combined with Moravia's, although the victory was dampened by the latter's death from wounds received in battle. In an unprecedented step, the nobles of Scotland created William Wallace Regent of Scotland.

The provocation increased in earnest. Edward could be relied upon to react, resolute to stamp out such opposition. At Falkirk, in 1297, Wallace's forces were soundly beaten, although guerilla warfare continued. Wallace is believed to have fled abroad for a period, possibly to rally support in France, but on his return in 1305, he was betrayed by Sir John Monteith, captured in Glasgow and taken for trial at Westminster. His monument in Union Terrace, Aberdeen carries an extract from the words he spoke at his trial, and, indeed these very words expressed the profoundest sentiment of his countrymen.

> "To Edward King of England I cannot be a traitor. He is not my king. I owe him no allegiance. He has never received homage from me and, while life is in this persecuted body, he never shall receive it."

Wallace was convicted of treason and thereupon dragged through the streets of London to Smithfield where he was hanged, drawn and quartered. His head was then displayed on a spike on London Bridge for all to see. The barbarous manner of Sir William Wallace's ignoble end was, one should appreciate, no more repulsive than many deeds perpetrated by that hero himself. What Edward in his fury failed to forsee, however, was that in meeting out such unsavoury justice, he had created a martyr. Scotland's cause took on a new and escalating significance. Many who had hitherto avoided commitment, flocked to the banner, including Robert Bruce, who, with the death of his father was now head of the House of Bruce and could act on his own behalf. Shocked at the news from Smithfield, his mind was made up at last.

And events moved dramatically fast for Robert Bruce. A meeting had been arranged with John the Red Comyn, Balliol's nephew, at Greyfriar's Church, Dumfries. The actual purpose of the meeting is unknown, but it is likely that it was to settle differences and endeavour to form a united front against the common enemy, Edward Plantagenet. Some say that a conspiracy with the English was involved, but the outcome was a violent argument between the two men in which Bruce stabbed Comyn to death, and thereby initiating a bitter feud surmounting that already existing between the two powerful families.

There was no time for delay. Bruce rode immediately to Scone aware that he had committed the ultimate sin; murder within a church.

Traditionally, earls of Fife had placed the crown of Scotland on the heads of each new Scottish monarch. On Palm Sunday, in the absence of her brother, the Earl, Isabella, Countess of Buchan, crowned Robert I of Scotland. Since the sacred stone and regalia had

*The Scottish Regalia which can be seen on display in the Crown Room at Edinburgh Castle.*

been removed, she extemporised with a plain gold circlet. The Abbots of Scone and Inchaffrey and the Earls of Monteith and Atholl were present. Also at Bruce's side was James Douglas, who was to prove himself his greatest friend and general, and whose family in successive generations were to grow as powerful as the Royal House itself, intermarrying and indeed, enabling a future Stuart king to claim the English throne. At Scone, Robert Wishart, Bishop of St Andrews, said mass and absolved the new king from his crime, but this could not prevent the Pope, under powerful pressure from England, from excommunicating him for having committed a sacrilege. Robert Bruce had arrived at the throne of his ancestors, but he had still to win his kingdom and the odds were stacked up high against him.

# *From 1306 to the death King David II*

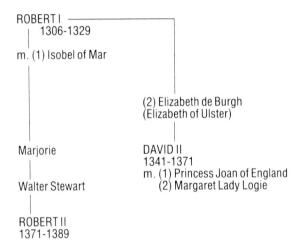

HOUSE OF BRUCE

ROBERT I —————————————┐
   | 1306-1329

m. (1) Isobel of Mar

                                     (2) Elizabeth de Burgh
                                     (Elizabeth of Ulster)

Marjorie                         DAVID II
                                  1341-1371
                                  m. (1) Princess Joan of England
Walter Stewart                      (2) Margaret Lady Logie

ROBERT II
1371-1389

# 4

## The Hero King

KING Robert I's greatest quality was dogged determination. Added to this was an ability to sustain terrible persecution and personal sadness without in any way weakening his resolve. There must, however, have been moments when, during those early days of tribulation, he must have wrung his hands in sorrow and contemplated the awful course of his destiny.

Immediately after the coronation, Wishart and the Bishop of Glasgow were seized by the English. At Methven, surprised by troops led by the Earl of Pembroke, Bruce's forces were defeated, the king forced to flee. Near Crianlarich he was attacked by Red Comyn's cousin, John MacDougall of Lorn and a swarm of his highlanders. One of these grabbed Bruce's mantle and, though mortally wounded, held it so tightly that the king was compelled to unclasp the brooch which fastened it. Known as "The Brooch of Lorn", this can be seen today at the MacDougall castle of Dunollie, Oban.

Hounded by his enemies, Bruce was on the run and headed north, where he had strong support from Munro of Foulis (despite his over-lord Ross), Kenneth of the Nose, Chief of Clan Mackenzie, and Angus, Lord of Islay, brother of the Lord of the Isles. Angus Og hid him at Dunaverty Castle from where he narrowly escaped to the Mackenzie stronghold of Eilean Donan on Loch Alsh. His movements from then on are not surprisingly vague. It is thought he sailed off to the Western Isles, possibly to Orkney. Later he was to be found on Sanda and then Rathlin Island, off the coast of Ireland.

Perhaps the most famous story of this period concerns Bruce's encounter with the spider who inspired him to "try, try and try again". It is said that this took place on Rathlin, although at

Kirkpatrick Fleming in Dumfriesshire there is a cave in which Bruce most certainly took refuge, sheltered by Irving, the owner of an adjacent house. Known as Bruce's Cave, it is hollowed out of stone on a cliff face and can be visited today by means of a narrow footpath.

Meantime, the Queen and the young Princess Marjorie had been sent to Kildrummie Castle in Aberdeenshire for safety. They were moved to the Sanctuary of St Duthac at Tain shortly before Kildrummie fell by treachery of a local blacksmith who, having been promised as much gold as he could carry, set fire to the castle. The garrison surrendered and its inmates, including Bruce's brother Nigel, were "hangyt and drawyn". The smith was rewarded by having molten gold poured down his throat.

The most powerful man in the North East at this time was William, Earl of Ross, once an inmate of the Tower of London, an adherent to the Comyn cause, and surprisingly anxious to seek approval from the English king. Seeing the chance of winning favour with Edward, Ross violated the Sanctuary, captured the Queen and Princess and handed them over to their enemies who carried them south. The Countess of Buchan, whose husband, being a Comyn, was bitterly opposed to Bruce, was also imprisoned for her part in the coronation ceremony. It seemed that all about him his friends and family were paying a terrible price for their loyalty. From Rathlin, however, Bruce emerged with renewed energy. He sailed to Lochranza on Arran en route for Turnberry. A further disaster occurred when Bruce's brothers Thomas and Alexander with an Irish Force were defeated by Sir Dugald Macdowall in Galloway. Their execution must have had a deep effect on the king, but then the tide began to turn.

At Loudenhill, Bruce, with only 600 men, defeated the Earl of Pembroke and his force of 6,000. The news travelled south to Edward Plantagenet who was, once again, outraged. Gathering together a great army he immediately set forth to crush the Scots once and for all. But although the English king's spirit was as iron as ever, he was now an old man and his stamina was failing. He died on the march.

The situation immediately changed. The new King Edward II was of a very different mould. The "Hammer of the Scots" last wish was that his bones be carried in a leather saddlebag so that he could still lead his army to victory. His son handed the bones to the Archbishop of York and after a half-hearted attempt to suppress opposition north of the Border, returned South.

Bruce was now on the offensive. Avenging his brothers, he

laid waste MacDowall's lands in Galloway and set about obliterating the Comyns in the north. Although suffering from a recurring infection, Bruce won victories at Slioch, near Huntly and at Barra Hill, where he defeated John, Earl of Buchan. Comyn lands and castles were distributed amongst Bruce supporters and the king turned his anger towards John of Lorne. Aided by Angus Og MacDonald, Bruce won the Battle of Inverurie and captured the MacDougall stronghold of Dunstaffnage. Angus Og's brother, Alexander of the Isles, who had supported John of Lorne, was captured and his lands and titles given to his younger brother. John of Lorne, meanwhile, fled to England.

Many would have expected Bruce to turn on Ross now, but instead the king accepted his surrender and homage. Many were indeed surprised when then the Earl was given Dingwall Castle and additional lands in Sutherland. Bruce no doubt had shrewd insight, for he was rewarded with life-long loyalty and the life of the Earl's son Walter at Bannockburn.

For the time being the English threat had died away. Edward II was preoccupied with his favourite Piers Gaveston, Earl of Cornwall, son of a Gascon knight, and a domestic power struggle with the English nobles, who despised Gaveston's arrogance and intimate influence over the king.

In 1309, King Robert held a parliament at St Andrews at which a peace treaty with England was proposed. Troop movements in the South continued to cause concern, but a temporary truce was nevertheless achieved even though English Garrisons were seen to be reinforced. In 1310, in a General Council at Dundee, the Clergy of Scotland reinforced their support by announcing their official recognition of their king. The Pope, however, remained indifferent. Aided by his surviving brother, Edward Bruce, the king set about liberating his castles — Linlithgow, Dumbarton and Perth. With Angus Og's assistance from the West, he captured the Isle of Man, although it was shortly afterwards reclaimed by their old enemy John of Lorne, who had been appointed England's Admiral of the Western Seas. In March 1313, Sir James Douglas surprised Roxburgh and Sir Thomas Randolph captured Edinburgh. Edward Bruce took Rutherglen and laid siege to Stirling, whose Governor, Sir Phillip de Mowbray agreed to capitulate if not relieved before the 24th June 1314.

In the meantime, Edward II had lost the struggle with his nobles; his beloved Piers Galveston had been taken and executed and regardless of how the English king felt about this, it was

imperative that he should seek to regain respect for the monarchy, and at the same time enforce his own position. With the whole available feudal levy of England, and a contingent from Ireland, he set out once more to invade Scotland. The army which advanced from Berwick numbered 20,000 men. On 22nd June 1314, they reached Falkirk.

Bruce's star was in the ascendant. At a preliminary skirmish, Bruce dazzled his own men by fighting a personal combat with Sir Henry de Bohun, whom he felled with a single blow of his famous axe. The next day the Battle of Bannockburn took place, and the result was to determine the independence of Scotland and to firmly establish Robert Bruce as King of Scots.

He had known his ground. He had chosen to fight between St Ninian's and a small burn known as the Bannock, which was surrounded by marshes dangerous to heavily armed horsemen. Bruce's troops were in four divisions: his brother on the right, Randolph in the centre and Douglas on the left. Bruce's Standard was planted at the Bore Stone, which presented the best view of the battlefield. Now the Scots at Bannockburn fought on foot in battalions with their spears facing outwards, in a circular formation. This could well have seemed a great handicap against armoured horsemen and the brilliant skills of the English archers. But a momentary triumph by the latter was quickly reversed by a flank movement from Sir Robert Keith. The Scottish bowmen followed up the advantage and the fight became general. The English horse, crowded together and bogged down in the marshy ground, found themselves at the mercy of the Scottish pikemen. The English rear, meantime, was unable to come up into the narrow fighting area. A rout turned into a headlong flight. Edward himself barely escaped, many of his great nobles including the Earl of Gloucester were killed and many hostages taken. It was these hostages who enabled King Robert to negotiate for the return of his wife and daughter from captivity.

At Ayr on 25th April 1315, by unanimous consent, the succession of the Scottish throne was universally determined as going to Robert Bruce, and, failing males of his body, to his brother Edward and his heirs male, or failing them, to Robert's daughter by his first marriage, Marjorie, and her heirs, if she

*The famous Pilkington Jackson head of King Robert I modelled for his monument at Bannockburn.*

married with the king's consent. Shortly after this event, Marjorie married Walter the Steward.

Robert Bruce had won his kingdom, but there was still much to do. To begin with he made generous provision for his supporters, but friction with England continued and there was the over-riding rejection by Rome.

In 1315, Edward Bruce crossed to Ireland on the invitation of certain Irish nobles and chiefs, and in 1317 Wales, Ireland and Scotland became allies. King Robert had joined his brother in 1316, crossed to Limerick and together won nineteen victories in the progress, although Dublin was saved by her inhabitants burning their city to the ground.

Success was too fast to endure, but nevertheless, Edward was crowned King of Ireland. When Robert returned to Scotland he received the news that a battle had been fought at Dundalk and his surviving brother had been killed. Such are the burdens of kingship.

Robert dedicated himself then to the siege of Berwick. Two Cardinals arrived meantime from the Pope with orders to effect a truce or, failing such, to renew Bruce's excommunication. Wary of crossing the Border, they sent their messengers instead, but Bruce refused to admit the papal bulls into his kingdom since they were not addressed to himself as king. A later attempt by Adam Newton, guardian of the Minorite Friars at Berwick was similarly dismissed. In March 1318, the town and castle of Berwick surrendered leaving the road open to waste the English Border as far south as Ripon.

In 1320, the Scottish Clergy and barons petitioned the Pope. This Declaration of Arbroath declared a Nation's undying loyalty to its king: "For so long as but one hundred of us shall remain alive we shall never consent to bow beneath the yoke of English domination". The Pope could not fail to be impressed at this remarkable testament of loyalty, but he still refused to revoke his ban.

Victories against English forces continued, although minor, but at Byland in 1322, King Edward was once again almost captured. This unfortunate king seemed doomed to failure in all aspects of his existence, culminating in his unsavoury murder at the hands of his wife's lover Mortimer in 1327. On hearing the news, Scotland wasted no time in invading England, and the young King Edward III was defeated at Stanhope in 1327.

The new English king had much to resolve and realised that in order to put his own realm to rights, peace with his northern neighbour must be achieved. A treaty at Holyrood therefore

*The Horn of Leys — King Robert I's hunting horn which can be seen at Crathes Castle, Aberdeenshire.*

recognised Bruce as King of Scots and England gave up all claims to that country. Finally that question was resolved. At Northampton in 1328, the English Parliament confirmed the Act, and as a gesture of goodwill, it was agreed that Bruce's son David should marry the Princess Joan of England, sister to King Edward III. Influence was brought to bear and in 1329, Pope John XXII officially recognised King Robert I of Scotland, lifted his ban of excommunication and authorised that henceforth kings of Scotland be crowned and annointed as rulers of an independent kingdom.

*King Robert I's sword, property of the Earl of Elgin.*

Bruce's achievement was complete, but his personal battle against the illness that had plagued him from the days of his early struggles, he lost. He passed his latter years at Cardross Castle on the Clyde. He made careful provision for his funeral and tomb. He arranged for a Papal bull authorising his confessor to absolve him even at the moment of his death. On 7th June 1329, at Cardross, King Robert I of Scotland died of Parylitic leprosy. He was buried at Dunfermline beside his second wife, Elizabeth de Burgh, daughter of the Earl of Ulster. In fulfilment of a vow to visit the Holy Sepulchre, Bruce had requested that Sir James Douglas, his greatest friend, carry his heart on a crusade to Jerusalem. Douglas himself, perished fighting the Moors in Spain, and the heart, recovered by Sir William Keith, was returned to Scotland where it was interred at Melrose Abbey.

Scotland has had no greater inspiration than Robert Bruce. His story serves as one of the greatest examples of patriotism and dedication to a cause at the expense of all personal consideration. His eventual triumph against constant seemingly insurmountable odds must surely be a lesson for all.

*From the brass over King Robert I's grave at Dunfermline Abbey where he lies buried beside his second wife, Elizabeth de Burgh.*

ROBERTI DE BRVS

SCOTORVM · REGIS · SEPVLCHRVM · RD · MDCCCXVIII · INTER · RVINAS

HOC · AERE · DENVO · CONSIGNATVM · EST · ANNO · POST · IPSIVS · OBITVM · LLX

PRVSTA · RETECTVM

King David II had been born at Dunfermline in 1324 and was therefore five years of age on his father's death. In accordance with the terms of the Treaty of Northampton he had married Princess Joan of England in 1328. His Coronation took place at Scone in November 1331, but already forces were at work to depose him.

Thomas Randolph, Earl of Moray took up the post of Regent with flair and held the country together with success until his death in 1332. Unfortunately, his demise coincided with the return of John Balliol's son, Edward, intent on claiming his birthright.

Although Edward III did not give Balliol any active assistance against his brother-in-law, Comyn supporters rallied to his cause. Balliol landed at Kinghorn, Fife in 1332 and shortly after won a major victory against Scots forces led by Donald, Earl of Mar, the new Regent, who was killed in action. The Battle of Duplin Moor enabled him to take Perth, and on 24th September he had himself crowned at Scone. His acknowledgement of Edward III's suzerainty won him that king's support, but shortly afterwards he was defeated by Bruce supporters at Annan and compelled to flee to England. With the back up of an English force, Balliol once again defeated the Scots at Halidon Hill in 1333, and as part of the deal surrendered the whole of Lothian to England, who immediately set about garrisoning large castles. Naturally civil war escalated, particularly when Edward did homage to the English king.

Steadily, the English were driven back, mostly through the efforts of the new Earl of Moray, and when David returned aged twenty one, lands north of the Forth were secure.

A call for support from the king of France was to be his downfall. In 1340, the young king invaded England and at Neville's Cross, near Durham was defeated and captured by his brother-in-law. David's step-nephew, Robert Stewart, however, escaped and returned home to become Regent.

Although he would probably have had things otherwise, David had a relatively pleasant time as a hostage, more his brother-in-law's guest. In the meantime, Scotland was torn with internal strife and corruption. In 1357, despite the depths of poverty to which his country had sunk, David succeeded in buying his freedom for 100,000 merks to be paid in ten yearly instalments, this despite the economic crisis prevailing in his country.

By this stage it might seem that David II's task in Scotland was impossible. His early record brought him little credit, although there were few who could knowingly criticise him. His subsequent relationship with his brother-in-law while that king's captive did not encourage adulation from a country that had fought a heroic guerrilla war on his behalf. And, is so often the case with sons of famous fathers, he would always be compared with Robert Bruce.

Yet King David II was a shrewd man with many of his father's qualities, not least an ability to be patient. The disorder of his realm brought about by years of unrest, warfare and exploitation, would have been a challenge to the wisest statesman. The Black Death ravaged the country, as did widesprad poverty. The stability of his throne was foremost a problem, particularly as he had no heir. David was not impressed by his step-nephew Robert Stewart, who had acted Regent, and even harboured plans that should he himself fail to produce an heir, the throne should pass to one of King Edward III of England's sons. This, of course, would never have been accepted.

In 1362, Queen Joan died leaving David free to marry his mistress, Dame Margaret Logie, widow of Sir John Logie, daughter of Sir Malcolm Drummond. Their match, however, also failed to produce an heir and David, aware that he was unable to meet the terms of his release from captivity, attempted a devious game, suggesting Lionel Duke of Clarence, Edward III's son, be recognised as his heir. The Scottish parliament naturally rejected the proposal, which was accompanied by a minor uprising in protest. David, however, was playing for time, and treated with his brother-in-law, at the same time seeking to have his marriage annulled so that he could marry one Agnes Dunbar.

The Queen, however, had other ideas. She had had a child by her first marriage and was unsympathetic to the king's claim that she was incapable of bearing another. In 1370, she took her case to the papal court at Avignon where she persuaded the Pope to reverse a decision taken by the Scottish bishops. The King, then, was unable to marry again and thus disappeared any hope of his fathering a legitimate heir. In February 1371, David died, last of the House of Bruce.

Under the terms of succession agreed by the Scottish Parliament in 1318, the throne now passed to Robert "The Steward", son of Princess Marjorie, twice Regent of Scotland during David's absence, and at the time of that king's death imprisoned with his four sons for opposing the proposed succession of the Duke of Clarence.

## The Stewarts
## 1371-1542

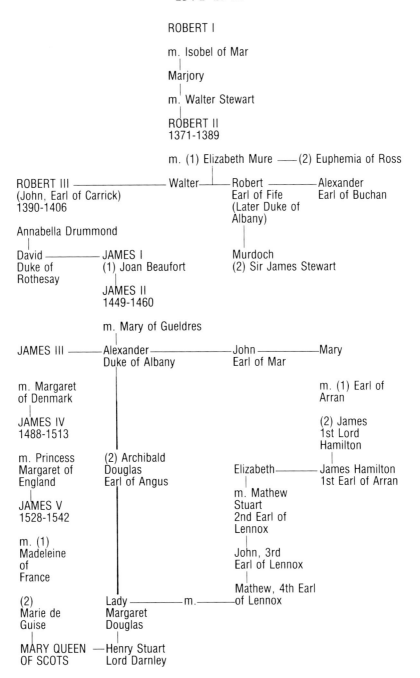

ROBERT I

m. Isobel of Mar

Marjory

m. Walter Stewart

ROBERT II
1371-1389

m. (1) Elizabeth Mure ——(2) Euphemia of Ross

ROBERT III ——————— Walter —— Robert ——————— Alexander
(John, Earl of Carrick)                    Earl of Fife        Earl of Buchan
1390-1406                                    (Later Duke of
                                            Albany)

Annabella Drummond

David ———————— JAMES I              Murdoch
Duke of            (1) Joan Beaufort     (2) Sir James Stewart
Rothesay
                   JAMES II
                   1449-1460

m. Mary of Gueldres

JAMES III ———— Alexander——————— John —————— Mary
                   Duke of Albany     Earl of Mar

m. Margaret                                              m. (1) Earl of
of Denmark                                              Arran

JAMES IV                                                 (2) James
1488-1513                                                1st Lord
                                                        Hamilton

m. Princess       (2) Archibald
Margaret of        Douglas             Elizabeth——————— James Hamilton
England            Earl of Angus                         1st Earl of Arran
                                       m. Mathew
JAMES V                                Stuart
1528-1542                              2nd Earl of
                                       Lennox

m. (1)                                 John, 3rd
Madeleine                              Earl of Lennox
of
France                                 Mathew, 4th Earl

(2)               Lady ———— m. ———— of Lennox
Marie de           Margaret
Guise              Douglas

MARY QUEEN —Henry Stuart
OF SCOTS           Lord Darnley

# 5

## The Stewarts

Lesser than Macbeth, and greater.
Not so happy, yet much happier.
Thou shalt get kings, though thou be none.
So all hail Macbeth and Banquo!

THUS Shakespeare's witches foretold the destiny of the unfortunate Banquo. But although the House of Stewart, by continued
tradition, originated from this so-called Banquo, Thane of Lochaber, they more credibly descended from a Breton (therefore Celtic)
noble, Alan, Seneschal of Dol.

The Seneschal, a crusader in 1097, died without issue, but his
nephew, Fitz-Flaald came to England with King Henry I and
became Sheriff of Shropshire. It was his third son, Walter, who came
to Scotland with Kind David I and was appointed High Steward.
Such was the way of things in the Feudal world that this office was
confirmed as being hereditary by King Malcolm IV.

In his book on King Charles I and II, *The Image of the King*,
Richard Ollard describes the Royal Stewart dynasty thus:

"From first to last, how they defy sobriety and probability.
Through the half-shut eyes of imprecise historical recollection, what
a stir of colour and movement, what drama, what pathos, what
inexorability. Mary Queen of Scots and Bonnie Prince Charlie are
but two of the major luminaries in this constellation. Escapes,
pursuits, imprisonments, disguises, sudden reversals of fortune,
plots, betrayals, loyalty and courage, how their story has differed
except in the last two particulars from that of the dynasty that has
supplanted them."

Of all the Royal Houses of Europe, the Stewarts were to prove to be the most prolific, the most disordered and certainly the most consistently turbulent. It was, however, the younger sons, the daughters and the natural children who, through their marriages and captivating charm, brought about glamour and chaos spreading into the courts of Europe.

But the man who began the Royal Stewart dynasty was in his fifties when he inherited his throne, and his eldest son and successor, having been injured in a riding accident, was far from being a powerful or impressive figure in the land. But King Robert II had six sons and seven daughters by his two marriages, and no less than eight illegitimate sons into the bargain.

On becoming king, although at a glance it would seem to have been straightforward, the question of Succession was Robert's prime concern. He had first married Elizabeth Mure of Rowallan, but later discovered that they were related, and so closely that a Papal dispensation was required to make the marriage legal. This indicated that children conceived before the dispensation was affected might be considered illegitimate.

After Elizabeth's death, Euphemia, daughter of the Earl of Ross became Robert's second Queen, and obviously the legitimacy of their subsequent family was beyond question. Determined that his eldest son should succeed him, however, Robert instigated an act of succession in 1373, by which John, Earl of Carrick and his heirs male should receive the crown, whom failing, the next son and his heirs male, and so on.

Robert Stewart had been Regent of Scotland twice in his career. He clearly saw David II's proposals to nominate the Duke of Clarence as heir as a slight against his own abilities and was obviously not privy to the political motivation. As a result of his righteous opposition, he therefore found himself and his family languishing in prison.

Although he had shown laudable skills in battle, government and in procreation, he seems to have gone rapidly into decline. He appears to have accepted his crown with little enthusiasm and in 1343, he handed over the powers of legislation to his heir. Six years thereafter, a tired recluse, he died.

Like his father, Carrick, who assumed the style of King Robert III, inherited in his fifties. He was preoccupied with religion, and it was popular superstition which prompted him to discard the name John, too closely associated with the House of Baliol. A kick from a horse meant that he walked with a limp, and, with his Queen Anabella Drummond, he preferred to lead a quiet life at Carrick Castle. Although he almost certainly attended several parliaments,

*Lochindorb in the bleak Morayshire moors and where the notorious Wolf of Badenoch made his headquarters in the 14th Century.*

he chose to become what amounted to the nominal ruler of Scotland, handing over the reins of government to his brother Robert, Earl of Fife, a very different mould of character who was later elevated to the Dukedom of Albany.

Another brother, Alexander, Earl of Buchan, controlled the Highlands. Appointed King's Lieutenant in the North in 1372, this wild individual had married the immensely wealthy and widowed Countess of Ross, a relative of his step-mother. It was apparent from the start that they loathed one another, and by mutual agreement they decided to live as far apart as was possible, she remaining at Dingwall Castle while he took up residence at Loch-in-Dorb with his mistress Mariota of Altyn.

Known as the "Wolf of Badenoch", Alexander imposed a reign of terror from his sinister, impenetrable island stronghold situated in the midst of bleak Moray moors. Surprisingly, he brought a level of order to a region where there had hitherto been little control. Perhaps the savage highlanders understood the rough justice of this King's Lieutenant. Like all Stewarts he was immensely prolific, and his many natural sons by Mariota and others were to found the

*The remains of 13th Century Elgin Cathedral, burned by the Wolf of Badenoch in 1390.*

Highland Stewart branches and to enable him to command what amounted to his own private army.

But his reputation and deeds inevitably brought him into conflict with his brothers, and his desertion of his wife led to his excommunication by the Bishops of Moray and Ross. He had a violent temper and in retribution, burned Elgin Cathedral, an act which outraged the nation.

Meantime, despite a fourteen year truce with England, Border warfare was constant. A French expeditionary force arrived in Scotland and King Richard II of England retaliated by burning Scottish Border Abbeys. Albany, nevertheless, held Scotland in an iron grip. But with the King's family growing to maturity, all knew that his powers were temporary, and in 1399 many welcomed the appointment of the King's eldest son as Lieutenant of the Kingdom. David, Duke of Rothesay, was an arrogant and impetuous youth, and doubtless Albany was deeply angered by the appointment, which he must have realised was inevitable. It was not long, however, before the two Dukes began to clash regularly in their opinions. Cold and ruthless, it was only a matter of time before the experienced Albany was able to hinder his nephew's advancement. Rothesay's incompetence was Albany's trump card.

In 1401, Albany succeeded in persuading his brother that Rothesay should resign his office, and when the Royal Command was refused, Albany saw to it that Rothesay was arrested. The King, seeing his son's actions as the affrontary of youth, took no action to prevent Rothesay from being imprisoned in Albany's Castle of Falkland. Not long after that the Prince was found to be dead.

Nobody could countenance that it could be murder, although the rumours spread about starvation. Albany was too powerful. Nobody could believe that he could risk such an outrage, and when a judicial enquiry took place, he was utterly vindicated. Nevertheless, King Robert III, from that point, became totally paranoid about the safety of his remaining son, James.

Although reluctant to accuse his brother, Robert could hardly fail to be aware of his brother's ambition. It was therefore decided in 1406 that the Prince should be sent to France for his education and safety. The boy was eleven years old and the King was in failing health. Justifiably, the king feared what might happen should he, himself, die and Albany take control.

The young Prince was therefore despatched on a ship, which, as fate would have it, was attacked by Privateers who saw advantage in handing the Scottish Prince over to King Henry IV of England.

A truce was in existence by now between England and Scotland, but the English decided to keep James prisoner, and, indeed, he remained one for eighteen years. King Robert III died shortly after hearing the news, possibly from the shock.

The young prince thus became nominal King of Scots while the government of the realm was continued by Albany, who showed little interest in procuring his nephew's release. In 1420, Albany died and was succeeded as Regent by his son, Murdoch, equally uninterested in his cousin's fate.

James meantime was moved about as if some plot to release him was anticipated. From the Tower of London he was removed to the Castle of Nottingham and then to Evesham. Over this period he was in the hands of capable tutors and began to show great promise both as a sportsman and as a scholar. In addition, he revealed a talent for music and considerable ability as a poet.

In 1413, Henry V became ruler of England and James was returned to the Tower of London, but not for long. The English king took it upon himself to welcome his cousin at Windsor and a warm relationship sprang up between the two kings. James even took part in Henry's French campaign, although possibly being used to draw off the Scottish auxiliaries fighting for France.

After Henry V's death, negotiations for James' release began in earnest. Scotland desperately needed a king to curb the rapidly growing civil unrest. In September 1423, a treaty was signed at York, the Scottish nation undertaking to pay a ransom of 60,000 marks, said to be for "his maintenance in England". By the terms of the treaty James was to wed a noble English lady, and it is fortunate that looking from his window one morning he saw and fell immediately in love with Lady Joan Beaufort, daughter of the Duke of Somerset, and great-grand-daughter of King Edward III of England. The match could not have been more suitable. It was to be a life-long love match and the lady's dowry contributed 10,000 marks towards his ransom. In April 1424, the exiled King and Queen travelled to Scotland.

Over the period of the Regency, great Scottish nobles — notably the House of Douglas in the South, Clan Donald in the North — had ruled their lands with unchallenged powers. Disputes were settled by judicial combat and for the main part concerning the acquisition or ownership of land.

James I was crowned at Scone on 21st May 1424 and immediately set about putting his country to rights. Statute Law based on the English system was introduced and with this additional emphasis assigned to government through parliament there began the process which would ultimately break down the power of the nobles. At the same time this was to work towards the eventual demise of ultimate sovereign power. "If God grant me life," announced the King, "though it be but the life of a dog, there shall be no place in my realm where the key shall not keep the castle and the bracken-bush the cow."

At Perth in March 1425, a Parliament took place and James took the opportunity to have the ex-Regent Murdoch, his sons Walter and Alexander, and his brother Duncan, Earl of Lennox, arrested.

*A likeness of King James I of Scotland (1424-1437), an extravagent monarch, but one who mastered his country.*

IACOBVS · I · D · GRATIA
REX · SCOTORVM

Without delay, the four were sentenced to death and executed at Stirling. This ruthless act emphasised that the King perceived the very real threat posed to the monarchy by his cousins. In addition, the Earl of Strathearn and James, Master of Atholl, descendants of Queen Euphemia's marriage were conveniently sent to England as hostages for the King's ransom.

James was determined to gain a strong grip on Scotland, and this meant the prevention of crime and suppression of both criminals and rebels against his cause. In 1426, he founded what was to become the Court of Session, presided over by the Chancellor and representatives of the Three Estates. To illustrate his egalitarian character, a 'poor man's advocate' was appointed to represent those who were unable to pay for their defence.

All this was very commendable, but in the Highlands there was much to be done. In 1427, King James held a parliament at Inverness and summoned every Highland chief of consequence to attend. Forty chiefs accepted in good faith and there followed an action which was to cause much bloodshed and opposition. Chiefs, on arrival, were separated from their followers, and on entering the Royal Audience Chamber, many were seized and several executed on the spot. Among those arrested were Alexander of the Isles and his mother, Princess Margaret, daughter of Robert II, and therefore, James' aunt. This lady spent most of her remaining days imprisoned at Inchcolm as hostage for her son's good conduct after his release. The action at Inverness was conceived as a means of strongly emphasising the power of the king, that law and order were being, at-long-last, restored. But at the same time, there were many who were outraged at the king's behaviour.

Within two years Alexander of the Isles had summoned together 10,000 men and marched on Inverness, which he burnt. The King marched north and a battle was fought at Lochaber. The Islesmen were defeated and the Lord of the Isles forced to surrender at Holyrood. Surprisingly, it was an intercession by Queen Joan that saved his life, but he was installed for a year or two at Tantallon Castle, the impregnable Douglas stronghold perched on the cliffs at North Berwick.

In 1436, King James I seemed to have mastered all Scotland. He had also squandered money on Linlithgow Palace, and on fine clothes, a throw back to his days at the English Court. He was

*Tantallon Castle on the cliffs near North Berwick, probably built by the first Earl of Douglas and later held by the Douglas Earls of Angus.*

generally popular, admired if not loved, but the old threat from the family of Euphemia of Ross was to materialise once again, and this time, tragically.

Walter, Earl of Atholl, was the younger son of Queen Euphemia and King Robert II. His son, the Master of Atholl, had been hostage in England, but had died there. In company with Sir Robert Graham, uncle of Malise, Earl of Strathearn, a plot was hatched in favour of Atholl and his younger son.

The King and Queen had chosen Perth as their favourite residence, and on the night of 20th February, they were staying at the Dominican Priory of Blackfriars. Despite the heroic action of one of the Queen's ladies, Catherine Douglas, who thrust her arm through the staples of the door in place of the missing iron bar, Sir Robert forced entrance and stabbed the king to his death. The Queen, wounded in her attempt to save her husband, managed to escape. At Holyrood, she first ensured that her six year old son was crowned King James II, the first Scottish king not to be enthroned at Scone, and then she set about the task of capturing her husband's murderers.

If Atholl had expected an immediate popular uprising in his favour, he was very wrong. The people of Scotland had forgotten the two families of King Robert II and only saw the brutal assassination of a respected king, whose son was rightful heir. The Queen's forces soon captured the plotters who, at the command of this fairest of Queens, were horribly tortured and put to death.

Once again Scotland was faced with the prospect of rule by a Regent. Queen Joan was undoubtedly a strong character, but turned to the fifth Earl of Douglas, a grandson of King Robert III. Two years later she re-married to Sir James Stewart, known as the "Black Knight of Lorne", and they had three sons who became John, Earl of Atholl, James, Earl of Buchan, and Andrew, Bishop of Moray. She died in 1445 and was laid to rest beside her first husband in the church of Charterhouse, Perth. Meantime, Douglas, assisted by Bishop James Cameron of Glasgow, as Chancellor, endeavoured to govern Scotland. An extraordinary power struggle then developed between Sir William Crichton, governor of Edinburgh Castle, and Sir Alexander Livingston, governor of Stirling Castle. Both sought power through holding the king's person, and both worked to destroy the power of the House of Douglas, and that of each other.

In 1438, Douglas died and was succeeded by his sixteen year old son, William, as sixth earl. Whether or not the ten year old king was

*A likeness of King James II (1449-1460), a child of six when he was crowned at Scone.*

IACOBVS 2 D GRA
REX SCOTORVM

party to the plot will never be known, but it is unlikely. Nevertheless, on 24th November 1440, the young Douglas and his brother were summoned to dine with their king and cousin at Edinburgh Castle. Sir Walter Scott tells us that a black boar's head was set in front of the Earl foretelling his doom, and at this 'Black Dinner' the two young men were seized and taken to be executed on Castle Hill. The young king, it is said, protested at this vile act, but there is little doubt that he learnt much about treachery at this time in his life and would not be averse to practicing similar deeds on reaching his maturity.

James, seventh Earl of Douglas, great-uncle of the two murdered boys, and known as "The Gross", seems to have played a shadowy role in this business, and now emerged as ally to the Livingston faction, working to undermine Crichton. While doing so, Douglas power was once again being reinstated, and it was natural that the young king should be aware that if his own position was to be secure, this must be checked.

King James II was aged nineteen when he married Marie of Gueldres, niece of the Duke of Burgundy. He was the survivor of twins and had been left with a facial discolourment which earned him the name of "fiery Face". As a consequence, the king avoided ceremony or public occasions, developing as a soldier king, intent on action. Scotland needed a strong man to reinstate firm government, and this was he. Crichton was discredited and it was not long before the Livingstons also fell. The Douglases were another matter.

James the Gross's eldest son, William, had succeeded and was eighth earl, commanding vast estates in the Borders stretching over to Galloway. In 1452, the King discovered that Douglas with the Earl of Crawford and the Lord of the Isles had made a traitorous allegiance with England, and this gave him the opportunity he required to act. Douglas was summoned to Stirling under safe conduct. After dinner, the king challenged Douglas with his treachery and demanded that he break his bond. Douglas refused and the King, supposedly in a fit of anger, stabbed the Earl and tossed his body out of a battlement window.

Parliament exonerated the King on grounds of the Earl's treason, but Douglas power was angered. William's brother, now ninth Earl, attacked Stirling with his brother's safe conduct document attached to the tail of his horse. What amounted to a civil war broke out in Southern Scotland.

King James II had shown considerable interest in the science of gunnery, and this was to prove an invaluable asset. Massive bronze cannons were cast and used to batter the walls of Douglas castles. Among these weapons was the celebrated 'Mons Meg', which can be

*Dirleton Castle, East Lothian, built in the 13th Century.*

seen to this day on the battlements of Edinburgh Castle. Overall such military equipment was well beyond the means of even a power as wealthy as Douglas. Only the treasury could justify the commissioning of such weaponry as being in the interests of the defence of the Realm. It was thus inevitable that the more powerful force should prevail. At the Battle of Arkinholm in 1455, Douglas power was crushed; the Earl himself fled to England, where he allied his services to the House of York coinciding with the outbreak of the Wars of the Roses.

It was a difficult time for England, but in Scotland it seemed that at last a situation of peace and prosperity had come about on which to build. Certainly influenced by Douglas' allegiance, James chose to support the House of Lancaster in the personage of King Henry VI

JACOBVS 3 D GRATIA
REX SOTORVM

of England, a fellow monarch. But the Scottish king had no intention of becoming embroiled in England's civil war. Being allied to Lancaster, however, justified an attempt to reclaim Roxburgh Castle, held by English forces since the 12th Century, and controlled by a Yorkist Governor. As had become the practice, James' cannon, freed from flattening Douglas strongholds, were to be employed under the King's personal supervision. It was during the action at Roxburgh Castle that one such weapon, over-charged with gunpowder, exploded, despatching the zealous king to his maker.

Queen Marie, on receiving the news, showed remarkable fortitude. Taking her nine year old son immediately to Roxburgh, she bravely demanded that her husband's memory deserved the tribute of a great victory. Scotland's army commanders re-commenced their siege with renewed vigour and within days the Castle fell. King James III was crowned in Kelso Abbey on 10th August 1460. Once again a Stewart child was monarch and a Regency inevitable. From the start, England hoped to exploit the situation and the successful Yorkist, King Edward IV, formed a treaty with the still exiled Douglas and the Lord of the Isles to partition Scotland and to rule as England's vassals. Shrewdly, the Regency took steps to abandon their Lancastrian pact and succeeded in affecting a truce with England thereby diverting the immediate danger. The young king, however, found himself facing a far greater threat when first his mother, Queen Marie, died in 1463, then his advisor, Bishop Kennedy of St Andrews died in 1465. Like his father, James III was to learn cunning in the interests of survival. But he lacked his father's ruthless nature, and once again an ambitious noble family was on the make.

In 1467, the young King was seized by Lord Boyd of Kilmarnock and the King's military tutor, Sir Alexander Boyd. These two brothers transported the king from Linlithgow to Edinburgh Castle, where they forced him to make a statement approving their action. The Boyds then set about making themselves the power in the land and arranging a marriage between James and Princess Margaret of Denmark, daughter of King Christian I of Denmark, Norway and Sweden. Norwegian claims in Orkney and Shetland were pledged against the Princess' dowry, and when the agreed sum was not forthcoming, Scotland acquired the Northern Isles, formally annexed in 1472.

To strengthen their own position, Lord Boyd's son was betrothed to the King's sister, Princess Mary. But the eighteen year old king remembered his father's example, and shortly after his marriage in 1469, seized Sir Alexander Boyd and had him executed. Lord Boyd and his son escaped into exile.

Unlike his father, King James III possessed considerable physical beauty and an artistic temperament, characterising him as a true Renaissance prince. While becoming a great patron of the arts, commissioning fine architecture, collecting classical papers, generally encouraging painting, poetry and the design of elaborate jewellery, he lacked the bite to dominate a restless, unruly land.

Above all, James III was a lover of peace, shunning the military interests of his father, and those with whom he surrounded himself had similar tastes. In consequence, many of his companions were not of noble birth and this, in itself, incited a snobbish reaction. His tendency to cultivate and promote favourites, several low-born, coupled with his aesthetic temperament not surprisingly gave rise to rumours of homosexuality, undermining the position of a King whose outlook was very much in line with the great flowering of culture elsewhere in Europe. And there was obviously some truth in the insinuations concerning the King. He did appear to champion intelligent male company, but at the same time, the King's marriage by all appearances was happy; the Queen, a devout and gentle woman, bearing him three sons. When she died in 1486, James petitioned the Pope to have her canonised.

As was now the pattern, the King's major problems originated from his immediate family. His brothers, Alexander, Duke of Albany, and John, Earl of Mar, were spirited, ambitious men, who found their brother lacking. There is little doubt that Albany, like his namesake and great-great uncle, aspired to the throne, and the two brothers were eventually arrested under suspicion of treason. Mar died in prison, but Albany escaped to France, and then to England, where he found a sympathetic King Edward IV. Once more, England offered support in return for Scotland recognising the English king as 'over-lord', and Edward acknowledged Albany as 'Alexander IV of Scotland'. An army under Edward's brother Richard, Duke of Gloucester, marched on Scotland, successfully capturing Berwick. James mobilised, but unwisely placed many of his favourites in key positions, infuriating many of those who had rallied to his support. Ill feeling reached such a pitch that when the Royal forces were encamped in the grounds of Thirlestane at Lauder, Archibald, Earl of Angus (to be known thereafter as 'Bell-The-Cat') with a group of nobles seized six of the King's closest advisors and hanged them in front of James off Lauder Bridge. Among the unfortunate victims were the musician William Roger, and Robert Cochrane, who had designed the great hall at Stirling Castle.

The Royal army retreated to Edinburgh, but when Albany arrived, no doubt having received word of the murders, his reception was not at all what he might have expected. It is probable that by this stage the Scottish nobles had had word of Albany's traitorous activities, and Albany was advised to reconcile himself with his brother, while the English army retired South. This development indicates that James must have possessed considerable diplomatic talent. Further diplomacy was evident when Albany was appointed Lieutenant of the Kingdom, but the following year he was found to be once more involved in treasonable negotiations and, in consequence, forced to flee again. Finally, in 1488, aided this time by Douglas, Albany invaded for the last time. His army was defeated at Lochmaben and Douglas captured and imprisoned while Albany fled once more to France where he later died.

The Tudors had meantime ascended the Throne of England, and James set about negotiating a cleverly conceived strategy for peace between the two countries. King Henry VII of England had married King Edward IV's daughter and it was proposed that James' eldest son, Prince James, should marry one of her younger sisters. To complete a triangle, James, himself, now a widower, would marry Edward IV of England's widow, Queen Elizabeth. With the two Royal Families bound so closely together surely peace would prevail.

Once again, however, the King of Scotland's subjects were becoming restless about the way his realm was being administered. It was natural that the traditional ruling houses of Scotland should resent the upstart manners of the King's low-born favourites such as Robert Cochrane. But although he had undoubtedly learnt his lesson from Lauder Bridge, James continued to promote handsome male friends to positions of responsibility, and it had become apparent that James' affections had been caught by John Ramsay of Balmain, a young man from a good family, whom he created Lord Bothwell. Once again a favourite's intimate influence with the King's affairs became bitterly resented by the Court, and once again it was 'Bell-The-Cat' who acted.

In 1488, aged fifteen, Prince James was seized by a powerful group of rebel noblemen with the purpose of using him to depose his father. Quite what the young prince's personal attitude to this was we will never know, but with such determined persuasion he had very little option. On 11th June, King James III of Scotland confronted an impressive army led by his own son at Sauchieburn, near Stirling.

The Royal army was overwhelmingly defeated and the King himself forced to flee from the battlefield. While escaping, his horse stumbled and the King was thrown to the ground. The story goes that the Miller of Bannockburn rescued the unconscious monarch and carried him to the nearby mill. The King, recovering consciousness, asked to see a priest. The Miller's wife set off in search of one and returned with a stranger claiming to be a priest. Instead of reading the last sacrament, however, this individual produced a knife, stabbed the King to his death and disappeared, causing great embarassment to the victors, who had never desired the King's death.

King James III, an intelligent but unpopular monarch, was laid to rest beside his Queen in the Abbey of Cambuskenneth, near Stirling. Their son, filled with remorse and guilt, for the rest of his life wore an iron link belt around his waist as penance for indirectly bringing about his father's murder. But in contrast with his father, the sixteen year old King James IV was immensely popular with his subjects. The Spanish Ambassador of the day, Signor Pedro de Ayala, described him as "handsome, highly educated and intelligent, active and effective". He had one major advantage over his predecessors in that coming to the throne he was of an age (and character) to immediately take over the reigns of government himself without the interference or ambitious influence of guardians. James, therefore, held supreme power right from the start of his twenty five years as king. In consequence, he was able to stabilise the economy, suppress upstart factions and mould his country accordingly. The first education legislation was introduced in 1496 demanding that all Barons, Chiefs and Chieftains take full advantage of the opportunities for learning available; that their sons should be encouraged to acquire "perfect Latin". Studies of literature and medicine flourished. The Royal College of Surgeons was granted its Charter in 1505. The printing press was introduced to Scotland for the first time in 1508; works of Chaucer and the poet William Dunbar were published. In this century three Universities were founded — St Andrews in 1411, Glasgow in 1451 and Aberdeen in 1495, the latter the result of collaboration between James and Bishop Elphinstone, formerly James III's Chancellor. James IV, we are told, spoke no less than eight languages, including Gaelic, and combined his father's intellectual and artistic enthusiasms with a love of sport, being both an excellent horseman and academic. Through shrewd management Crown Revenues doubled, although large amounts were spent on armaments and the building of a powerful fleet to police the Western Highlands and Islands. His flagship The Great Michael, built at Newhaven in 1511, was reputedly the largest ship of its time.

*King James IV (1488-1513) who reluctantly married Margaret Tudor after the murder of his true love, Margaret Drummond.*

ACOBVS·4·D·GRATIA
REX·SCOTORVM

Expenditure on building was no less ambitious. At Linlithgow, work on the Palace was commenced by Andrew Aytoun in 1496; similarly work on Falkland and Holyrood began.

At the same time James discovered that he could use the full powers of patronage at his disposal to great advantage. Stewart kings had always had these powers at their disposal, but had never really turned them to profit. The Crown could confer titles, land, pensions, offices at will. In addition, the Pope had conceded the right to nominate candidates to high offices in the church, and this simply added to the king's powers to win friends and influence people. James loved to travel about his land personally overseeing local justice, making himself known to his subjects on extensive visits, on pilgrimages to Whithorn in Galloway or the Shrine of St Duthac at Tain. Sometimes the Court went with him, sometimes he travelled alone, becoming something of a mythical figure, moving incognito among his people.

James stayed twice at the Castle of Dingwall, summoning his Chiefs to attend him. The intense love built up between the Highlanders and their ruler, an extension of the Clan to Chief principle, came about at this time. James professed a great affection for the northern parts of his realm, and the Stewart loyalties he forged were to endure until the virtual annihilation of the Clans took place at Culloden over 200 years later.

Such sexual insinuations as had been levelled against James III could never have been made against his son, who showed an almost excessive and traditionally Stewart interest in womankind. The tall red haired King had four mistresses who bore him five children. The King's marriage, however, was a very different affair.

Early on King Henry VII of England had made efforts to unsettle his neighbour's throne, certain that only turmoil could follow Sauchieburn. Ramsay of Balmain was encouraged to kidnap the young King, but the plot failed, and Ramsay, forfeit of his Belhaven title, fled to England.

England, however, was still reeling from the Wars of the Roses, and James retaliated by sponsoring the Yorkist pretender Perkin Warbeck, whom he proclaimed 'Richard IV of England'. Although Warbeck spent two years in Scotland under James' protection and an invasion was mounted, England had had enough of civil strife; nobody rose to support the cause and the invasion was a failure.

Nevertheless, Henry VII was impressed enough to offer James his daughter's hand in marriage as a peace token. For James, however, the gesture had little appeal. For some time he had had it in mind to marry his mistress Margaret Drummond, daughter of John, 1st Lord Drummond. Indeed, it is said that they were, in fact, already married, and she had borne him a daughter, also named Margaret. Daughters of Drummond had been wives to David II and Robert III, and there was certainly a degree of jealousy about this in high circles, although this was not now a significant reason for opposing such a match. Even the King must have realised that marriage with the King of England's daughter would bring untold benefits of peace and prosperity. Matters, however, were taken out of his hands when in 1502 Margaret and her two sisters were found to have been poisoned at Drummond Castle.

James, stunned by the death, agreed to marry Margaret Tudor, who became his Queen aged thirteen in 1503. It is said that neither party had much enthusiasm for the other. Margaret was frequently homesick, although she bore her husband six children and by most standards lived a full and spirited life both before and after James' death.

Although signing a Treaty of Perpetual Peace with England, James held firm to the 'auld alliance' with France. Politically this was a means of maintaining an independent voice alongside England, but it could only be sound providing that England remained at peace with France. James' conviction at this juncture was that the forces of Christendom should assemble against the Turks, who were threatening Central Europe. Others saw things differently.

Pope Julius II had spent his early career endeavouring to oust the powerful Papal family of Borgia. His aim was to restore, consolidate and extend the temporal possessions of the church and by a series of devious and diplomatic moves he reconciled the powerful Italian houses, arbitrated on the differences between France and Germany and concluded an alliance with them to oust the Venetians from the Italian towns they occupied. In 1508, Julius concluded against Venice the League of Cambray with the Emperor Maximilian, Louis XII of France and Ferdinand of Aragon. The following year the city of Venice was placed under an interdict. By the Battle of Agnadello, the Italian dominion of Venice was virtually lost, but when the allies were not satisfied with merely affecting his purposes, but intent on taking matters further, Julius made an about turn and entered into a pact with the Venetians against his now former allies. He absolved Venice in 1510, and shortly after placed an interdict on France. At Tours, before Louis XII, French bishops announced their withdrawal from Papal authority. Julius next formed the Holy League with Ferdinand and Venice against France. Thus, ultimately, the Emperor Maximilian and England were brought into a war against France.

At one stage James and Julius must have stood on good terms as the Sword of State, part of the Scottish Regalia, a rich Italian

masterpiece, was a gift from the Pope in 1507. But James, nevertheless, bitterly reproached Pope Julius for dividing Christendom and received an order of excommunication in reply. The involvement of James' brother-in-law, King Henry VIII, in the light of future developments, was particularly ironic. In 1513, England invaded France, who appealed to Scotland for help. James initially despatched his Lyon Herald to Flanders with an ultimatum. Henry scorned the message, re-asserted England's feudal superiority and stated that on his return he would "expulse" his brother-in-law. A man of honour, James had no alternative but to declare war despite an apparition which appeared to him at the Church of St Michael, Linlithgow warning him against such action. It is an indication of James IV's personal following that he was able to assemble the largest united army Scotland had ever seen. They came from farthest corners to muster at Borough-Muir, outside Edinburgh. The exact size is open to speculation — it was estimated that 40,000 assembled, although only around 30,000 crossed the Border. These included the 23-year-old Archbishop of St Andrews (James' natural son by Marion Boyd), 15 earls, 20 barons and hundreds of knights. All were well equipped, well fed and hardened fighting men. In addition, Louis XII had sent 50 French soldiers under Count d'Aussi along with money, wine and weapons. James' cannon left Edinburgh Castle pulled by 400 oxen, ammunition carried by 30 pack horses.

On August 22nd 1513, the Scottish army crossed the River Tweed at Coldstream, raised Castle Wark and marched downstream to Norham, crossing the Till at Twizel Bridge. Norham fell after a siege of six days and the army proceeded South to Etal. Ford Castle was held by Lady Heron in the absence of her husband, who had been taken hostage for his natural brother John who was to act as a vital guide in the English flanking operation. Some say that she allowed herself to be seduced by James so that the Scottish advance should be delayed. Whether or not there is any truth in this, she was rewarded when James burned her castle to the ground before departing.

But the fact that the Scots had advanced only 4 miles into England in 14 days seems to suggest that James had no intention of fighting a pitched battle. He possibly hoped for a brief encounter affording him the excuse to withdraw into Scotland, thereby honouring the alliance.

It was after mid-day when scouts reported that the English were across the River Till, and bearing down from the North. Trumpets

*A likeness of King James V (1528-1542), seventeen months old when he inherited the throne after the disastrous Battle of Flodden.*

sounded and troops assembled, while orders were given for the cannons to be moved from their emplacement and dragged to Branxton Hill, a position from which James considered it possible to command the Pallinsburn crossing.

Infantry followed, forming up along the crest of the hill. On the left was the Earl of Home and his Borderers who usually fought on horseback, but were formed into pike columns. Accompanying them were the Earl of Huntly's Highlanders, and to their right were forces from Perthshire, Angus, Forfar and Fife under the command of the Earls of Errol, Crawford and Montrose. In the centre was the King with the Earls of Cassilis and Glencairn, with Lord Herries and Lord Maxwell. Behind were positioned the Earl of Bothwell and troops from the Lothians. On the far right were positioned the Highland forces under the Earls of Argyll and Lennox.

The weather was appalling, visibility very poor and undoubtedly caused considerable shock to the English army who suddenly came upon the entire Scottish army at a distance of less than half a mile through the mist. Sadly this was not to Scotland's advantage.

In a period of two hours, Scotland's finest army was obliterated. King James IV lay dead amid some 9,000 or more of his subjects. Among them was almost the entire ruling class of Scotland.

It was with some difficulty, indeed, that Lord Dacre, and the captured Chamberlain, Sir William Scott, next day identified the King's body. It had been stripped naked by looters, had a deep cut from ear to ear and one hand was severed. Wrapped in what remained of the Royal Standard, it was laid in the Church of St Paul's, Branxton, before being taken to Berwick-on-Tweed to be embalmed. From there, the Earl of Surrey escorted the body to London where it was buried in an unmarked grave at St Michael's Cornhill. Being an enemy of the Pope, he was denied a Christian funeral.

The disaster was such that many Scots refused to believe that it had taken place. If anything, amid all the confusion, the reaction was almost hysterical. The Provost of Edinburgh rallied the City to prepare for attack, but he need not have worried for the English, content with their carnage, drew back. A myth sprang up that the people's beloved King of Scots had gone on a pilgrimage to Jerusalem. One day he would return, and the legend became akin to that surrounding King Arthur of Camelot. James IV was the "Once and Future King" who would one day re-appear to put his country to rights again.

To this day the Battle of Flodden is remembered each year during Coldstream's Festival week in August. Coldstreamers ride across the fine River Tweed bridge past Cornhill-on-Tweed to Pipers Hill, where a wreath is laid at the foot of the Flodden Memorial. Then the Cavalcade of horses, led by the "Coldstreamer", gallop up the hill to Flodden Edge where an annual service is held and an oration delivered by a prominent Borders figure.

> *Their King, their Lords, their mightiest low,*
> *They melted from the field as snow,*
> *When stream are swoln and south winds blow,*
> *Dissolves in silent dew.*
> *Tweed's echoes heard the ceaseless plash,*
> *While many a broken band,*
> *Disordered, through her currents dash,*
> *To gain the Scottish land;*
> *To town and tower, to down and dale,*
> *To tell red Flodden's dismal tale,*
> *And raise the universal wail.*
> *Tradition, legend, tune and song*
> *Shall many an age that wail prolong;*
> *Still from the sire the son hear*
> *Of the stern strife and carnage drear,*
> *Of Flodden's fatal field,*
> *Where shivered was fair Scotland's spear,*
> *And broken was her shield!*

Sir Walter Scott
*Marmion.*

Once again a child inherited the Scottish throne. King James V was but seventeen months old when he was crowned at the Chapel Royal, Stirling in 1513. His widowed mother had been appointed guardian under the terms of her husband's will, but as the sister of King Henry VIII and openly recognising her brother as over-lord, this was hardly acceptable to the remaining nobles of the land. It was to the King's cousin, John Stuart, Duke of Albany, exiled with his traitorous father in France, that they turned.

Remarkably, John Stuart was a totally honest man, and while vested interests struggled to gain power, succeeded in preserving the independence of the kingdom without abandoning the 'Auld Alliance'. Arriving in Scotland in 1515, his appointment coincided with a treaty signed between England and France, and including Scotland. In 1521, Albany negotiated the Treaty of Rouen by which James V was to marry a daughter of King Francois I of France.

Queen Margaret's life after her husband's death became a series of intrigues, at one time in favour of England, then in favour of Scotland. She was an outstandingly selfish lady, at all times putting her own financial interests before those of her son and adopted country. Four of her children by James had died in infancy,

although a son was born posthumously but died a year later. Various projects for her re-marriage had started almost immediately after Flodden. Both Louis XII and the Emperor Maximilian had been candidates, but the Queen astonished all by marrying with almost indecent haste Archibald Douglas, Earl of Angus in 1514, less than a year from being widowed. In consequence, she alienated most of her powerful nobles such as the Earls of Home and Arran, and once again Douglas power was a force to be reckoned with. Albany had had to blockade the Queen in Stirling Castle before she would surrender her sons. Having done so, she returned to Edinburgh Castle and being no longer responsible for the custody of the King she fled to England where she bore Angus a daughter, the Lady Margaret Douglas, who, on maturity, was to marry the Earl of Lennox and be mother to Lord Darnley. It was through this connection that the kingdoms of England and Scotland were to be ultimately united.

In 1516, Margaret went to her brother's court in London while Angus, much to her displeasure, returned to Scotland, where he made peace with Albany and was restored to his estates, which included his impregnable Castle of Tantallon. Rivalry between French and English factions in Scotland escalated, being complicated by private feuds between the Hamiltons and the Douglases, headed by Arran and Angus, both contending for power in the absence of Albany, who had been summoned to France.

Margaret meantime quarreled with her husband over money matters and sided with Arran and then began to instigate divorce proceedings. When Albany returned he supported her divorce, but was accused of having designs on marriage with her himself. It was even suggested that he had become her lover until, once again, Albany found it necessary to retire to France, this time to take part in the Italian wars on behalf of King Francois I.

The Queen Mother had, in fact, fallen in love with Henry Stewart, second son of Lord Avondale, who she married immediately after her divorce in 1527. Margaret and her new husband, created Lord Methven, then became the ruling influence with the young King, and if anything is to her credit, it is that she resisted her brother's scheme to take James to London, where he could be kept under his Uncle's thumb. She did, however, try and arrange a meeting between the two, which led to James' accusation of her betraying him for money and acting as an English spy.

*Falkland Palace in Fife, completed by James V, who established a court for 'real tennis' here.*

In 1526, Angus had seized the King and kept him under close confinement until he escaped in 1528. At Stirling he put effective measures into effect against the Earl, who found it necessary to flee over the Border. The King was now in his late teens and playing a progressively stronger role in the affairs of his realm. The Borders had continually been a problem with damaging raids taking place on both sides, and since the King of England was, after all, the King of Scotland's uncle, negotiations for peace began in earnest.

It had consistently been Henry's plan that James should marry his daughter Mary, but the Scottish King turned his eyes to France, and in 1537 travelled to Paris to be married to King Francis I's daughter Madeleine. Sadly the young Princess died shortly after she reached Scottish soil, and in 1538, James, aged 22, married Marie, daughter of Claude, Duke of Guise, and widow of Louis d'Orelans, Duke de Longueville.

The outcome of these French alliances was that James placed himself defiantly against his Uncle, whom he refused to meet at York in 1536. Henry, meantime, had become entangled with church reformation thus ostracising himself from the Church of Rome. The gift of a cap and sword from Pope Paul III to King James V of Scotland did not serve to improve the relationship between uncle and nephew.

James endeavoured to follow his father's example. It is said that he was cold and ruthless, and no doubt, as virtual hostage to Angus, he had learnt the lessons of survival. He trusted few people, and consequently this red haired king with his steel-blue eyes earned few friends with the nobility upon whom he counted for support. Indeed, the harshness of his disciplinary measures made him both feared and despised.

In 1539, there was an uprising by Donald Gorm of Sleat, seeking to claim the Lordship of the Isles. Clashing with the Mackenzies and the MacLeods, Donald besieged Eilean Donan Castle, but was struck by an arrow which hit him in the leg and severed an artery which proved fatal. James took the opportunity to visit the Western Isles, where he stayed at Duntulm Castle with Donald's young heir. Having visited Orkney, the King sailed down to Dunbarton accompanied by a good many prisoners which he had decided would serve

*Lady Margaret Douglas, daughter of Margaret Tudor by her marriage to Archibald, Earl of Angus. In 1544, she married Mathew Stewart, 4th Earl of Lennox, and their eldest son, Lord Darnley, was destined to become husband to Mary Queen of Scots. It was through this union that King James VI could lay claim to the throne of England.*

*A painting at Falkland Palace of King James V (the "Gudeman of Ballengeich") and Mary of Guise, parents of Mary Queen of Scots.*

as hostages for the good behaviour of the Highland chiefs. Additionally, he decided to annex the Lordship of the Isles for the Crown.

Despite his high handed manner towards his nobles, James cultivated a strong following among the lesser people of his land. Like his father he would often travel among them, and quite often disguised himself as a simple farmer, in order to listen to what they had to say. This practice was obviously discovered as he soon gained the nickname of 'The Gudeman o'Ballengeich'. The King undoubtedly was able to see his people's problems at first hand, but whether or not he was able to do anything directly about them is debatable. By opposing the nobility, 'The Gudeman' was forced to turn to the Church, but a wave of Protestant belief was filtering through Europe intent on change. Papal approval enabled the King of Scots to levy £10,000 per annum on Scottish prelates to endow a 'College of Justice'. At the same time, James introduced his five illegitimate sons as lay abbots, which did little to strengthen the Church, but then, as was the habit of monarchs of that age, he believed that the Church and the Crown were indestructibly linked.

Queen Marie bore two sons who died in infancy. As such there was no heir to the throne and relations with England were deteriorating rapidly. Henry had attempted to persuade James to accept his religious policy, or at least, to remain neutral to it. In 1542, unreasonably, England invaded. The English force was led by the son of the victor of Flodden. James rallied his nobles, but they were reluctant to attack the English, and scattered. A second army was raised, commanded by Oliver Sinclair, and then James, himself, was taken ill.

The news of Scotland's defeat at the Battle of Solway Moss fought in Cumberland reached the ailing King at Lochmaben Castle. James seems to have experienced a complete nervous and physical collapse at this point, and, although he succeeded in reaching Falkland, died soon after.

On his deathbed he would have heard that Queen Marie had given birth to a daughter, Mary at Linlithgow Palace on 8th December. By then, James had become convinced that nothing would stop his uncle from over-running Scotland. Bemoaning the fate of the Stewarts, his dying words must have sounded sourly prophetic: "The Devil go with it. It came with a lass and it will go with a lass". The throne had come to the Stewarts through Marjorie Bruce, and he saw his six day old daughter as the last of the line. But that unhappy Queen was to prove him wrong, although all the social and religious undercurrents which had been building up throughout his reign would sweep her without mercy to her own personal tragedy.

# Mary, Queen of Scots

## 1542-1587

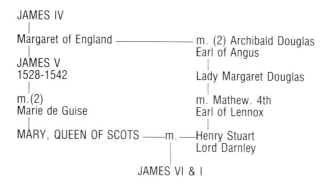

JAMES IV
|
Margaret of England ——————— m. (2) Archibald Douglas
|                                                       Earl of Angus
JAMES V
1528-1542                                     Lady Margaret Douglas
|
m.(2)                                        m. Mathew. 4th
Marie de Guise                      Earl of Lennox
|
MARY, QUEEN OF SCOTS ——m. ——Henry Stuart
                                       Lord Darnley
                            |
                   JAMES VI & I

# 6

## Mary, Queen of Scots

THE Queen Dowager considered it vital that precautions be made to strengthen the French alliance and consolidate the forces of Catholicism against the rising tide of Protestant worship. Many had expected King Henry VIII's army to sweep into Scotland, but that King was a superstitious man and had been cursed on his nephew's death bed. This did not prevent him from attemping to gain control of Scotland peaceably, and by the Treaty of Greenwich, it was agreed that the young Queen of Scots should marry Prince Edward of England.

A rising star in the land was the unscrupulous Cardinal Beaton who, collaborating with the Queen Dowager, who came of a powerful French family, arranged that the Treaty be discarded in favour of an alliance with the French throne. Conveniently, King Henry II of France's Queen, Catherine de Medici, had given birth to a son. A betrothal was quickly arranged, infuriating Henry VIII, and necessitating that the little Queen be kept under strong guard at Stirling Castle.

England invaded in 1544 and 1545, laying waste the Borders and Lothian. In 1546, Cardinal Beaton, a notorious persecutor of Reformers was murdered with English support, but primarily to avenge the death of George Wishart whom Beaton had burned for heresy at St Andrews. England's invasions were not outstandingly successful, although they wrought havoc, and in 1547, Henry VIII died. In that year, the Duke of Somerset, as Protector of England, and on the young King Edward VI's behalf, marched yet again on Scotland and inflicted a major defeat on the Scots forces at the Battle of Pinkie, just south of Edinburgh. Mary was urgently despatched to the island of Inchmahome in

*Mary of Guise, a portrait by Antonio Moro. As Queen Dowager, she held Scotland for her infant Catholic daughter against the rising tide of Protestant faith.*

the Lake of Menteith, where she was kept safe by the Augustinian monks in the Priory founded in the 13th Century. It was not to be a long stay before she was discretely transferred to Dumbarton Castle en route for France.

In August 1548, the six year old Queen Mary of Scotland landed at Roscroft, near Brest, on the Coast of France. The French Court in which she was to spend the next thirteen years had reached the heights of debauchery, immorality, murder and outrageous behaviour having full licence in the glittering, brilliant circles of Queen Catherine de Medici. To begin with, the French, and notably her betrothed, were enchanted by the little girl with the almond-shaped eyes. But the undercurrents of political intrigue ran deep.

King Henry II of France was obsessed with his mistress Diane de Poitiers, and the Italian Queen Catherine maintained a magnificent facade despite her constant humiliation. After ten years tutelage under a woman whose main instrument of policy became the corruption of her own children, Mary, aged 15, was married to the oldest and feeblest, two years her junior, in 1558. With the dramatic turmoil of her later career, one is inclined to overlook the fact that Mary Queen of Scots, as wife of King Francis II of France, was, for one year, also Queen of France. The same year as their marriage, the young Princess Elizabeth of England succeeded as Queen of that country.

The alliance between Scotland and France had never seemed stronger. But at home, the Queen Dowager, endeavouring to protect her daughter's interests, was coming into conflict with the new religion, the "Congregation of the Lord" embodied in the person of an ex-galley slave, John Knox. French troops found themselves repelling a combined force of Scottish and English allies from the walls of Leith, and in 1560, in Edinburgh Castle, the Queen Dowager died.

On 25th August 1560, Protestantism was declared the religion of the Scottish people, and Catholics were suppressed by a convention of states assembled without the assent of an absent Queen. The following year King Francis died from an abscess in his ear. It was to a sullen, antagonistic Scotland that his widow chose to return.

Now Mary had grown up with the seductive glamour of the French Court; the light-hearted frivolous behaviour of her upbringing was instantly at odds with the stern, moral and altogether pleasureless doctrine of Protestant faith as interpreted by such men as Knox. The heavy mist which shrouded Leith on her arrival from France was hardly welcoming. There was no reception, and had not Andrew Lamb, a local tradesman, offered shelter, it would have been an altogether unpleasant experience for the nineteen year old Queen.

Eventually her half-brother, James Stewart, whom she created Earl of Moray, and her Secretary of State, William Maitland of Lethington, arrived on horseback. Her own horse had died in transit, and the best that could be found was a sickly nag which shocked her French followers. A Queen of France should never be so wretchedly served.

As the Royal party approached Edinburgh they encountered an angry mob which had broken into a nearby jail to rescue one James Kellone, who had been sentenced to death for indulging in games on a Sunday. Mary was amazed at the severity of the sentence and immediately pardoned Kellone, her first decree on Scottish soil. The crowd cheered her, but she had unknowingly struck her first innocent affront to Calvinism, and it was to become a battle she could not possibly win.

On reaching Edinburgh at last, a welcome was evident with bonfires lit on the surrounding hills to salute her arrival. But Mary could not help noticing the poor, drab streets of her Capital.

Surviving portraits of Mary reveal her as a taught, rather severe beauty by modern standards. But to contemporary eyes, there can be no doubt that her fair skin, auburn hair and vivacious French mannerisms had instant appeal, although not, one suspects, to the religious leaders who sought to suppress sexuality and libidinous living. And despite claims that she failed to acquire the administrative qualities of a monarch, she began well enough with her advisors Moray and Maitland, seeking a conciliatory compromise with the Church in order to retain her personal Mass, at the same time recognising the reformed religion. Unlike her cousin Elizabeth, as a Catholic, Mary could not become earthly head of her country's established, reformed Church. The Scottish church thus developed independent of the Crown, a General Assembly evolving in which the three estates of Clergy, the Nobility and Burgesses were represented.

Surprisingly, it was other matters which required greater diplomacy. It was Maitland's concern that since Queen Elizabeth remained unmarried, Mary, as grand-daughter of Margaret Tudor, should be recognised as her heir. Furthermore, Elizabeth, as daughter of King Henry VIII's second marriage, was not recognised as legitimate by the Catholic Church.

Marriage became an all important issue in the two Courts; Elizabeth, while not exactly encouraging suitors herself, had strong ideas concerning a suitable match for her cousin. But then she was by no means ecstatic when Mary announced that she planned to marry their mutual cousin Henry Stuart, Lord Darnley, son of Lady Margaret Douglas, Countess of Lennox, and thus also a grandchild of Margaret Tudor. Any child of this liaison would have an indisputable claim to the Throne of England. The Lennox Stuarts were of the Stewart line, but having been domiciled for a period in France, the spelling of the name had altered. Darnley, having been brought up in England, had had occasional aspirations towards the thrones of both countries, and, in effect, Queen Mary's choice of husband was immensely

*Mary Queen of Scots — a "taught, rather severe beauty by contemporary standards".*

88

*A portrait of Henry, Lord Darnley with his younger brother, Charles, in 1563.*

shrewd, if not exactly romantic. Not that Darnley lacked good looks or manly charm. He stood over six foot and she is said to have described him as "the best proportioned long man we have seen". Unfortunately, he was to reveal himself as vain, arrogant, tactless and drawn towards personal excess. This might not have mattered had he not hungered for the political power which Mary, advised by Moray, denied him. As outlet for his frustration, he rallied similarly excluded nobles and the climax came when he accused Mary's Italian secretary, David Rizzio, of unsuitable familiarity towards his mistress.

One evening in March 1566, Darnley, the Earl of Morton, Lord Lindsay and Lord Ruthven burst into Mary's little supper room at Holyrood where she was dining with, among others, Rizzio. The unfortunate scribe was dragged through to the audience chamber where, at the head of the staircase, he was despatched with fifty-six dagger wounds. A plaque on the floor now marks the spot where his blood is said to have been spilt. The Queen, six months pregnant with Darnley's child, never forgave her husband for this dreadful deed.

Three months later, Prince James was born. His parents' marriage, however, had gone drastically into decline, and Darnley had scarce helped the situation by embarking upon a path of dissolute self-indulgence. Increasingly Mary was seen in the company of James Hepburn, Earl of Bothwell, who had acted as Admiral of the Fleet of the ships which had brought her from France. A rough man, a Borderer, he was a nephew of the Bishop of Moray and six years her senior. It was an unlikely match, but then he was in such contrast to the effeminate Darnley.

Mary's alluring power over men, if totally unconscious, was to lead her into constant difficulties. Early in her reign she had been hotly pursued by the poet Seigneur Montmorency d'Amville, son of a Constable of France, and more unhappily by Montmorency's attendant, Pierre de Boscose de Chastelard, also a poet. The latter, being found under Mary's bed at St Andrews was summarily executed.

Sir John Gordon, a swashbuckling character and third son of the 4th Earl of Huntly, had also had aspirations towards marriage, or at least, a liaison with the Queen. Gordon power in the North-East had reached excessive limits, and not for nothing had their Castle of Huntly become known as the Palace of Strathbogie. Huntly himself was a grandson of the 3rd Earl by a natural daughter of King James IV and could have been said to have risen somewhat beyond his station in his attitude towards his cousin. In 1562, Mary had marched North, ostensibly to combine a formal Royal visit with an attempt to curb Gordon influence. All along the route, however, she found herself having to fend off Sir John, who seemed intent on abducting her. At the Royal Castle of Inverness, she was refused admission by the Governor, another son of Huntly. Although his intention might not have been particularly serious, the purpose to persuade her to visit Huntly Castle, Mary interpreted his refusal as open rebellion. Gaining admission by force, she had the governor hanged from the battlements.

The Gordons had made a serious miscalculation. On reaching Aberdeen, Mary outlawed Huntly and his family. A fight was urged, the Countess of Huntly having been advised by witches that her husband would that night lie unscratched in Aberdeen's Tolbooth. At Corrichie, 15 miles west of Aberdeen, the forces met and the Earl promptly captured, whereupon he suffered a heart attack and died. Later his body was embalmed, taken to Edinburgh and formally tried for treason. Sir John, also captured, was executed with Mary as spectator. Ironically, Bothwell was married to Lady Jean Gordon, sister of the Earl of Huntly, but then affairs of state and rebellion had little to do with personal relationships or family.

Lord Darnley did not attend the christening of his son at Stirling Castle, He had retired to Glasgow where he had taken to wearing gauze over his face to hide a syphilitic rash. He seemed even to have lost his reason, suspecting, of course, that Mary was seeking to be free of him. In consequence, he wrote to King Philip of Spain requesting assistance in a bid to become sole ruler of Scotland.

A reconciliation seemed unlikely, and yet Mary succeeded in persuading Darnley to return to Edinburgh to discuss matters. The wedding of one of her favourite servants was taking place, and it became known afterwards that a quantity of gunpowder had been purchased by the lawyer Sir James Balfour and stored in his brother's house known as Kirk o' Field, close to Holyrood, where Darnley was to lodge for the night. The Queen was expected to attend the wedding ceremony, and while the celebrations took place, the plotters were able to finalise their plans.

In the early morning of Sunday 9th February 1567, a massive explosion destroyed Kirk o' Field. The bodies of Lord Darnley and his page were found in night attire, but curiously showed no signs of their deaths having been caused by the effects of the explosion. It was officially construed that they had both died from suffocation, and, therefore, deliberately murdered.

Shortly afterwards Mary received a letter from her Cousin Queen Elizabeth.

*Madam,*

*My ears have been so astounded and my heart so frightened to hear of the horrible and abominable murder of your husband and my own cousin that I have scarcely spirit to write: yet I cannot conceal that I grieve more for you than him. I should not do the office of a faithful cousin and friend, if I did not urge you to preserve your honour, rather than look through your fingers at revenge on those who have done you that pleasure as most people say. I counsel you so to take this matter to heart, that you may show the world what a noble princess and loyal woman you are. I write thus vehemently not that I doubt, but for affection.*

*Elizabeth R.*

History asserts that Mary was party to the plot from its inception. This, and the validity of the so-called Casket Letters which so conveniently disappeared, we will never know. Certainly, she is reported to have appeared stunned by the news. Bothwell, it was reported, had been seen leaving the scene of the crime shortly before the explosion. And it did not help that Mary now openly consorted with Bothwell, showering him with gifts while supposedly deep in her forty days of mourning.

An inquest was held and Bothwell indicted, but was later acquitted as having no part 'of the slaughter of the king'.

On 15th May 1567, Mary married Bothwell, who had divorced his wife. It is certain she was pregnant by him since she miscarried of twins in July. For any other reason it was madness, inciting intense opposition from her nobles and subjects.

Bothwell took Mary to Borthwick Castle in Midlothian, which was almost immediately surrounded by Confederate Lords led by Lord Home, once a supporter of Bothwell. Mary was forced to escape disguised as a pageboy. At Musselburgh, at Carberry Hill, the fugitives came face to face with the main army of their opposition. The Earl of Glencairn sent a message stating that if Mary disassociated herself from Bothwell, they would reinstate her as their rightful sovereign. Mary refused, but not wishing for bloodshed, then asked about the terms of her surrender. The rebel General Sir William Kirkcaldy of Grange replied that if she should surrender to him, Bothwell could go free. She agreed. It was as if the whole country had totally turned against her. At Edinburgh she was received by an ugly mob demanding revenge. Incited, no doubt, by the Church, they cried out "Burn the adultress!" It was considered unsafe for her to remain in the city

*Borthwick Castle, Midlothian, where Mary Queen of Scots fled with the Earl of Bothwell.*

and that very night she was taken to Lochleven Castle, home of Margaret Erskine, who had been her father's mistress and Moray's mother.

At Lochleven, Mary remained a prisoner for 11 months in the custody of Lady Douglas. Her treatment was unsympathetic and she was in poor health. On July 23rd 1567, pressured by Lord Lindsay and Robert Melville, she signed a deed of abdication in favour of her one year old son. At the same time she appointed her half-brother, Moray, as Regent. Over this period, a number of attempts were made to free the Queen. But ultimately, it was her own personal charm which unlocked the prison door.

Lady Douglas' two young sons, George and William, became

94

*Lochleven Castle, Queen Mary's prison for under a year.*

quite infatuated, and on 2nd May 1568, while other residents of the castle were at prayer, secured the keys, placed the Queen in a small boat, and having locked the gates behind them threw the keys over-board. On the shore, she was met by Lord Seton and Sir James Hamilton and taken to Niddry Castle, from whence she fled to Hamilton Castle.

For the time being, safe, Mary wrote to her half-brother stating that she had signed her abdication under duress and demanding that he relinquish the Regency forthwith. Furious that she had been allowed to escape, he naturally refused. At Langside, near Glasgow, Moray's 4,000 men defeated the Queen's army of 6,000. Heartbroken at seeing Scot kill Scot, the

Queen fled the battlefield. She spent a night at Terregles House with Lord Herries, and then, from Kenmure, the home of the Laird of Lochinvar, she rode to the Cistercian Abbey of Dundrennan. Here she was advised to go to France, but chose instead to cross the Solway and throw herself on the mercy of her cousin, Queen Elizabeth. It was a reckless, ill-conceived move, but she had no desire to return to France where her welcome was equally uncertain. Besides, Queen Elizabeth had for years shown a great interest in her Northern cousin, although they were destined never to meet. Sir James Melville of Halhill, an envoy to the English Court, recorded his impressions in 1564.

*She (Queen Elizabeth) appeared to be so affectionate to the queen her good sister that she had a great desire to see her. And because their desired meeting could not be so hastily brought to pass, she delighted to look upon her majesty's picture. She took me to her bed-chamber and opened a little desk wherein were divers little pictures wrapt within paper, and their names written with her own hand upon the papers. Upon the first that she took up was written, 'My Lord's picture'. I held the candle, and pressed to see that picture so named. She was loath to let me see it; at length my importunity prevailed for a sight thereof and found it to be the Earl of Leicester's picture. I desired that I might have it to carry home to my queen; which she refused, alleging that she had but one picture of his. I said again that she had the original; for he was at the farthest part of the chamber, speaking with secretary Cecil. Then she took out the queen's picture, and kissed it; and I kissed her hand, for the great love I saw she bore to my mistress.*

Melville's record also gives us a valuable insight into the two women.

*She (Queen Elizabeth) desired to know of me what colour of hair was reputed best; and whether my queen's hair or hers was best; and which of them two was fairest. I answered that the fairness of them both was not their worst faults. But she was earnest with me to declare which of them I thought fairest. I said she was the fairest queen in England and ours the fairest queen in Scotland. Yet she was earnest. I answered that they were both the fairest ladies of their courts and that her majesty was whiter, but our queen was very lovely. She enquired which of them was of highest stature. I said, our queen. Then, saith she, she is too high, and that herself was neither too high nor too low. Then she asked what kind of exercises she used. I answered that when I was despatched out of Scotland, the queen was lately come from the Highland hunting; that when she had leisure from the affairs of her country she read upon good books, the histories of diverse countries, and sometimes would play upon the lute and virginals. She asked if she played well. I said, reasonably for a queen.*

*I was earnest to be despatched, but she said I was weary sooner of her company than she was of mine. I told her majesty that though I had no reason of being weary, it was time to return. But I was stayed two days longer, till I might see her dance, as I was informed. Which being done, she enquired of me whether she or my queen danced best. I answered that the queen danced not so high or disposedly as she did. Then again she wished that she might see the queen at some convenient place of meeting. I offered to convey her secretly to Scotland by post, clothed like a page, disguised, that she might see that queen, as James V had gone in disguise to France with his own ambassador, to see the Duke of Vendome's sister, who should have been his wife; telling her that her chamber might be kept in her absence as though she were sick, and in the meantime none to be privy thereto, except my Lady Stafford and one of the grooms of her chamber. She appeared to like that kind of language, and said, 'Alas, if I might do it'.*

One wonders if history might have progressed differently had they met. Instead, Mary journeyed from one prison to another, and to one in which she was to remain for nineteen years. Her eventual participation in a Catholic plot to overthrow Elizabeth, on this basis, might therefore find some justification, and whether Elizabeth willingly and knowingly signed her death warrant is another truth which will never be known. Mary Queen of Scots' defence was that one monarch could not be condemned for an act of treason against another monarch. She was executed at Fotheringay, near Sheffied, on the 8th February 1587.

And what of Bothwell? To begin with he had taken refuge in the Orkneys, indulging in activities closely allied to piracy. His enemies, however, were close behind him, so he fled to Norway, then Denmark. In Copenhagen he appealed to the King of Denmark, who, not finding any immediate use for him, had him imprisoned at Dragsholm. Here, in 1578, he died, supposedly insane.

# JAMES VI & I
## King of two kingdoms

MARY, QUEEN OF SCOTS
1542-87

m. (1) King Francis II of France
    (2) Lord Darnley

JAMES VI of Scotland
    I of England
1566-1625

m. Princess Anne of Denmark

Henry ———— CHARLES I ———— Elizabeth

# 7

## King of Two Kingdoms

A WEEK after the death of his mother, King James VI of Scotland received a letter from Queen Elizabeth I of England.

*My dear Brother,*

*I would you knew (though not felt) the extreme dolour that overwhelms my mind, for that miserable accident which (far contrary to my meaning) hath befallen. I have now sent this kinsman of mine, whom ere now it hath pleased you to favour, to instruct you truly of that which is too irksome for my pen to tell. I beseech you that as God and many more know, how innocent I am in this case: so you will believe me, that if I had bid aught I would have bid by it. I am not so base minded that fear of any living creature or prince should make me afraid to do that were just; or done, to deny the same. I am not of so base a lineage, nor carry so vile a mind. But, as not to disguise, fits not a king, so will I never dissemble my actions, but cause them show even as I meant them. Thus assuring yourself of me, that as I know this was deserved, yet if I had meant it I would never lay it on others' shoulders; no more will I not damnify myself that thought it not.*

*The circumstances it may please you to have of this bearer. And for your part, think you have not in the world a more loving kinswoman, nor a more dear friend than myself; nor any that will watch more carefully to preserve you and your estate. And who shall otherwise pursuade you, judge them more partial to others than you. And thus in haste I leave to trouble you: beseeching God to send you a long reign.*

> *Yours most assured loving sister and cousin.*
> *ELIZABETH R.*

This almost motherly letter must have been an ironic comfort to a King whose own mother had offered him little affection, although this had not entirely been her fault. Elizabeth's concern is touching, one hopes not devious, reflecting a sympathey between two desperately vulnerable people on the death of a third, hopelessly so. But Elizabeth need not have been too concerned since her Scottish cousin and probable heir had developed into a strangely complex and unscrupulous individual determined, above all, to hold on to the throne of his ancestors at any price.

King James VI had been crowned at the Church of the Holy Rude, Stirling at so early an age that he would hardly have been aware of what was taking place. But the ceremony was conducted using the newly conceived Protestant rites, and, as such, was a triumph for the Reformed Church. To begin with, the child was put under the protection of John Erskine, Earl of Mar, while his step-uncle, Moray, as Regent, ruled the land on his behalf.

At Stirling Castle, the young King was placed under the tutelage of George Buchanan, considered a great scholar, but at the same time a tyrannical disciplinarian. It was he who instilled the virtues of a Classical education into the boy; Latin and Greek, but in particular, the Calvinist interpretation of the Bible.

> "His mind he must cultivate with sedulous care, his body as reason demands . . ." wrote Buchanan of his pupil.

At the same time, at every opportunity, the name of his mother was blackened. Buchanan loathed his former Queen, although strangely, earlier in his career he had dedicated a translated psalm to her. His admiration, it seems, had vanished on Darnley's death.

But James to his advantage had an independent mind. Although kept much alone, he rationalised theories of his own, particularly in regard to the Divine Right of Kings, which the Reformed church held severely in question.

In 1570, the Regent Moray, while riding through Linlithgow, was shot from a nearby building. The assassin was James Hamilton of Bothwellhaugh, a member of the Queen's still active supporters. Almost immediately, James' grandfather, Matthew, Earl of Lennox, was summoned to take his place. Lennox was popular with Elizabeth, but in order to keep control of any

*The infant King James VI of Scotland, illustrating an early interest in falconry.*

situation which might arise, his wife, Lady Margaret Douglas, the English Queen's aunt, was held in England as hostage.

Moray's death served to emphasise that a minor civil war was still in progress. Lennox set about strengthening his grandson's party. He took Dumbarton Castle, which had been held by the Queen's supporters. The next objective was Edinburgh Castle, held by Maitland of Lethington and Kirkcaldy of Grange, the latter having been won to the Queen's side after receiving her surrender at Carberry. A campaign was opened with James Douglas, Earl of Morton in command, but not long after, Maitland and Kirkcaldy attacked Stirling catching the defenders of that Castle unprepared, and although the attackers did not achieve very much, the Regent Lennox was shot in the back before he could be rescued.

The Earl of Mar was appointed next Regent and the war continued until there was a temporary truce in the Summer of 1572. The Queen's supporters began to disperse and eventually Edinburgh fell. Mar journeyed to Edinburgh to convene the lords of council, stopping on his way at Morton's mansion at Dalkeith. Here he was taken violently ill, compelling him to return immediately to Stirling, and where, shortly afterwards, he died. Many suspected that Morton had poisoned the Regent.

Morton was a rough, uncouth man who had acquired his title through marriage from his father-in-law. He was a devout supporter of the Reformation, committed to the English alliance, and had been involved in both the murders of Rizzio and Darnley, although there was no specific proof concerning the latter event. He was the survivor of those nobles who had been involved politically in the Reformation, and for a period was able to exercise immense power over Scotland. But all such men fall, and this fierce man, puffy faced with his great beard and cold eyes was to be no exception.

In 1579, there arrived at the Scottish court a young man of striking good looks. He was Esme Stuart d'Aubigny, the King's second cousin who had been brought up in France. At the age of thirteen, King James VI became infatuated with this talented, handsome kinsman. And he was hardly to blame. The young king had known nothing of friendship. He had been fatherless since birth, taught by Buchanan, a vociferous misogynist, pressured to despise his mother, and constantly in the company of the Royal Household's ladies, presided over by the overbearing Countess of Mar. He had become an accomplished poet, and it is interesting to note one such work which dismisses womankind in no uncertain terms:

*The Regent Morton — a "rough, uncouth man" who dominated the young King James.*

Even so all women are of nature vaine,
and can not kelp no secret unreveild,
and quhair as once they do conceave disdaine,
they are unable to be reconciled,
fulfillid with talk and clatteris but respect,
and oftentymes of small and none effect.

Ambitious all without regaird or schame,
but any measure gevin to gread of geir,
desyring ever for to winn a name
with flattering all that will thaime not forbeir,
sum craft they have, yit foolish are indeid,
with liyng quhyles esteiming best to speid.

It is not surprising that Esme Stuart, considered in France as one of the most handsome men in Europe, and bringing with him the gallantry and courtly mannerisms of the French court, should dazzle a lonely, unworldly if intelligent, teenager in search of affection. The fact that Esme Stuart, next to the King's elderly uncle, Lord Robert Stuart, was his nearest male relative, made his companionship unquestionably suitable. Much is made of King James' physical appearance. It was said that he was ugly, that his introverted shyness caused him not to look directly at people, that his tongue was too large for his mouth causing him continually to stutter and slobber. Yet visitors to the Scottish court reported that the King danced with "a very good grace". In later years it was said that he was clumsy and ever taking support from others. From his portraits, however, we see that he had light brown hair, sad grey eyes which were heavy lidded, and which reveal a certain intelligent mistrust. One suspects that the King affected physical mannerisms as he did mental eccentricities to aid him in the confusion of others. Not for nothing did he become known as "The Wisest fool in Christendom".

Utterly captivated then, King James created his cousin Duke of Lennox. With Captain James Stewart, a second son of Lord Ochiltree, the new Duke set about engineering the downfall of Regent Morton, and succeeded in doing just that by resurrecting information concerning Morton's involvement with Darnley's murder. Morton was found guilty and executed by the "Maiden", a guillotine which he himself had invented as a suitable way of disposing of his enemies.

Now Lennox was a Catholic, although agreeing to reform, but inevitably it was not long before it was put about that he was in Scotland to affect the restoration of Mary. James naturally dismissed the idea, but he was still under age, and in 1582, while out hunting, he was seized by a group of Protestant Lords led by William Ruthven, Earl of Gowrie. Lennox was forced to flee to France, where the following year, he died, a reformed Protestant, refusing last rights from a Catholic priest, and thereby, perhaps, paying James the greatest compliment. It underlined that the sentiment between the two men was mutual. James was heartbroken, but discovered, as he grew towards his seventeenth year, an inner strength and determination to free himself from the tyranny of such men as Gowrie. He was well acquainted with the histories of his Stewart ancestors who had freed themselves from their restrictions in their late teens. He thus determined to assert his rights and seize the powers of monarchy which were justly his and his alone.

In June 1583, aided by Lennox's friend, Captain James Stewart, the King escaped from Falkland Palace. It would seem that the conspiring lords were by now convinced he was unlikely to try and escape, and he was therefore not heavily guarded. Meantime, a group of noblemen — Huntly, Atholl, Eglinton, Bothwell, Rothes, Seton and Maxwell — were ready to support him against the Gowrie faction. James Stewart was created Earl of Arran. Gowrie was later taken prisoner and executed for his insult to the King's person. From the start of his personal rule in 1585, James began working towards a closer bond with England. At the back of his thoughts he constantly aspired to being recognised as Queen Elizabeth's heir. The following year, aided by his Chancellor, John Maitland of Thirlestane, a formal league was established, but although Elizabeth granted James a pension of £4,000 per annum, she repeatedly refused to officially recognise him as heir. Their relationship, however, continued to improve, and then the Babbington plot was revealed leading to the execution of Mary.

Heads of State cannot think as ordinary people. Whatever James' feelings about his mother, whom he had never known out of infancy, he was involved in an intricate power game. While Mary lived, there was always a possibility that she would return; indeed, there were many of his subjects who would have welcomed her. At the same time, she was arguably next in line to the throne of England. On receiving the news, he sent off a strongly worded message of protest, but that was all. In later years, as King of England, he built his mother a splendid tomb at Westminster and destroyed the castle at Fotheringay, no doubt to salve his conscience.

In 1588, England was pre-occupied with the Spanish Armada. James, balancing his Protestant nobles off against his Catholic nobles, remained neutral. The threat passed by and diplomacy prevailed. The following year, with Queen Elizabeth's approval, he journeyed to Oslo to marry King Frederick of Denmark's daughter, Anne, a girl of fifteen. Although pretty with her blonde Scandinavian looks, she was not outstandingly intelligent, which hardly altered his already conceived attitude towards women. She loved frivolous things; clothes, dancing, baubles, but it transpired that they were happy enough together. He became surprisingly possessive and she bore him seven children, although four died in infancy.

As early as 1585, James had commenced his attempts to have the church of Scotland controlled by bishops subject to the Crown. The attitudes of the two sides were clearly expressed when the formidable Andrew Melville, as Protestant spokesman declared that the King was 'God's sillie vassal'. James retorted simply, 'No Bishop, no King'. Although the King was ultimately to have his way, bishops becoming Crown servants, by that time James was firmly ensconced in the South of England.

Despite his learning, James was a surprisingly superstitious man, and least admirable of his obsessions was an upsurge in the persecution of witchcraft. Maybe it was all part of an inspired political strategy to distract his subjects, but many unfortunates died as a result. His cousin, Francis Stewart, created Earl of Bothwell after his Uncle's forfeiture, may have aspired to the throne, but his implication in the 'North Berwick Witches' scandal led to his leaving the country and death in exile. One is never sure with James; so many curious half-facts emerge making us speculate on hidden political intrigues.

An event which gives rise to such thinking took place in 1600 when, according to James, he was enticed by Alexander, Master of Ruthven, to Gowrie House, Perth, ostensibly to view some captured foreign treasure at the request of the Master's brother, the Earl of Gowrie. The King alleged that he was skillfully detached from his retinue and taken to an upper room where he was threatened and an attempt made to bind his hands. James, however, cried for help from an open window and in the ensuing fracas, both Gowrie and Ruthven were slain. In the light of the evidence available, the story appears highly implausible, but is typical of this elusive, anomalous monarch.

Queen Elizabeth I of England died in 1603, to the end not choosing to nominate an heir, but undoubtedly realising who that heir would be. James had been in regular correspondence with her chief minister Robert Cecil, and the road to the South was now wide open. Scotland had achieved over England what England had never achieved over Scotland. A King of Scots was now to become King of England.

And if James wasted no time in journeying over the border, he could hardly be blamed. He looked to the richer, calmer pastures, weary of the constant plotting and intrigues of Scottish government. In later years he wrote: "This I may say of Scotland, and may truely vaunt it: here I sit and govern it with my pen. I write and it is done, and by a Clerk of the Council I govern Scotland now, which others could not do by the sword."

King James VI, as he took his leave, promised to return. He found the ways of England very much to his liking, although his reign there was not altogether a success. Sadly for Scotland,

James did govern Scotland with his pen, and it was a precedent which was to have long term consequences for his predecessors.

From England he sought to dictate to the Protestant Church. Andrew Melville, summoned to London in 1606, was imprisoned for three years in the Tower of London. James returned only once more to Scotland, in 1617, and this was to impose the 'Five Articles' which proclaimed that Holy communion should be received while kneeling; that the Festivals of the Christian year should be celebrated; that confirmation be performed by bishops; and that private baptism and communion should not be permitted in cases of grave sickness. The reaction was violent. The King nevertheless insisted that the General Assembly held at Perth in 1618 should accept the Five Articles, but had the sense not to insist that they should be scrupulously adhered to.

King James VI and I died in March 1625. His absence strangely had made his Scottish subjects grow fonder of him, and curiously, since he had chosen to leave them, he was regarded to the end with a surprising degree of affection. Scotland had prospered. The excesses of his Court in England were out of sight. They would miss the "Blessed King James".

# *Absent Kings*

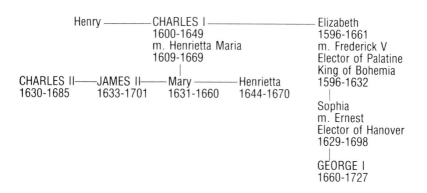

Henry ———————— CHARLES I ————————————— Elizabeth
                1600-1649                                  1596-1661
                m. Henrietta Maria                        m. Frederick V
                1609-1669                                 Elector of Palatine
                                                          King of Bohemia
CHARLES II——JAMES II——Mary————Henrietta    1596-1632
1630-1685    1633-1701  1631-1660   1644-1670
                                                          Sophia
                                                          m. Ernest
                                                          Elector of Hanover
                                                          1629-1698

                                                          GEORGE I
                                                          1660-1727

# 8

## Absent Kings

IN the absence of a resident monarch, it is surprising how Scotland maintained its loyalty to the Crown, but the kingdom which Charles I inherited in 1625 had prospered. Many of James' policies were to cause immense problems for his son, but it should be said that the King had always the option of compromise, which, one suspects, the canny King James would not have hesitated to exercise. Unlike his father, Charles was rigidly inflexible, and, of choice, removed from the mood of his people. He had been born the second son, suffering from delicate health and a speech defect. Like his brother and sister, he had been born in the Palace of Dunfermline, and had been taken to England at the age of three. Although involved in state politics for years before his father's death, it had been a priviledged existence very remote from the tangled intrigues and miseries of his father's youth.

We are familiar with Charles' likeness from the remarkable series of portraits executed by that great painter, Sir Anthony Van Dyke, a pupil of Rubens. He was a small man, immaculately attired, but it is a sad face, one which one cannot imagine smiling. A well known description by Sir James Weldon describes him thus:

> *He was naturally of a timid disposition, which was the greatest reason of his quilted doublets. His eyes large, ever rolling after any stranger came in his presence, inasmuch as many for shame have left the room, being out of countenance. His beard was very thin; his tongue too large for his mouth, and made him drink very uncomely, as if eating his drink, which came out into the cup on each side of his mouth. His skin was as soft as taffeta sarcenet, which felt so because he never washed his hands — only rubbed*

*A betrothal painting of King Charles II's natural son, the Duke of Monmouth, and the Buccleuch heiress.*

> *his finger-ends slightly with the end of a napkin. His legs were very weak, having had, as was thought, some foul play in his youth, or rather before he was born, that he was not able to stand at seven years of age — that weakness made him ever leaning on other men's shoulders. His walk was ever circular, his fingers ever in that walk fiddling about his codpiece.*

A rather acid description of this humourless, melancholy man, perhaps unfair, as certainly he proved himself a fine horseman during the Civil War, and towards his end displayed a great dignity.

Charles' marriage to a French Catholic Princess, Henrietta Maria, shortly after becoming king, greatly alienated his Presbyterian and Anglican subjects. Fears of a return to "Popery" filtered through the countryside. In 1633, Charles journeyed to Scotland to be Crowned in the Chapel of Holyrood House, ordering that English rites be used. To the staunch upholders of the Church of Scotland it was a direct affront.

Somehow Charles had come to the conclusion that he should bring the Scottish Church in line with that of England. Although this had always been James' intention, he had shrewdly not pressed the matter too far. In 1625 Charles had introduced an Act of Revocation. On reaching the age of 25, it had been the practice of Scottish kings to revoke grants made during their minorities. Charles, however, revoked all grants of Church lands made since the Reformation, an extraordinarily ill-conceived and provocative measure.

Coinciding with his visit, Charles announced that he, in company with his Archbishop of Canterbury, William Laud, intended to revise the Scottish liturgy. The proposal was explosive. An Anglican inspired service book to replace John Knox's Book of Common Order was quite unacceptable. On its introduction at St Giles, there was a riot; uproar broke out throughout the land. The King refused to receive Petitions and moved his Privy Council, through whom such Petitions should be made, to Linlithgow to avoid pressure from the Edinburgh mob. The Estates of Scotland were united in their opposition.

In February 1638, Charles announced that all supplications and convocations on the subject, in regard to his will were illegal. The people rose up and on February 28th 1638, the National League and Covenant was drawn up, based on James VI's 1581 Negative Confession of Faith drawn up against Catholics. At Greyfriars' Churchyard, Edinburgh, nobility, clergy and burgesses appended their signatures defiant to their King. But although the Covenant attacked Catholicism, rejected Anglican ideology in place of established Presbyterian practice, it underlined widespread loyalty to the Crown.

At a General Assembly of the Kirk held in Glasgow in 1638, James, 3rd Marquis of Hamilton, acted as Royal Commissioner with instruction to make a settlement with the rebels. The Assembly would not be moved from their entrenched position, so Hamilton dissolved it, but not before they had insisted on the deposition of all Scottish bishops.

At this assembly two men emerged as allies in their opposition to the crown — the Earl of Argyll and the Earl of Montrose.

With the King resolutely against compromise, the Assembly had no choice but to assert their decisions by force. Royal strongholds were seized and at Berwick, a Royalist force of 8,000 men under Charles faced a Covenanters force of 21,000 under Montrose and Alexander Leslie. By the Pacification of Berwick, the King surrendered to all the rebels' demands thus terminating the First Bishop's War. In future, all disputes between King and Covenanters would be referred to a General Assembly and Scottish Parliament. But the King was now faced with a new situation. An English Parliament had not met since 1629. The King's servants, the Earl of Strafford and Archbishop Laud were universally unpopular, but it was necessary to call a parliament in order to find funds to support the King's military action. The "Long Parliament" which was returned in 1641 impeached both Strafford and Laud, executing the former while sending the latter to the Tower of London. Faced with the threat of Civil War, the King found it politic to appease the Covenanters and appeal to Scotland for help. Visiting Edinburgh, he approved the General Assembly's 1638 motion to abolish episcopacy and the Revised Prayer Book and agreed that the Scottish Parliament could challenge his ministers. Alexander Leslie was created Earl of Leven, and the Earl of Argyll was raised to a Marquessate.

The King had conceded matters too late. When Civil War broke out in England, the Scots did not rally to his side. But as the Royalists won their early battles, the Parliamentarians made approaches for Scottish support and found that the recently created Marquess of Argyll was receptive.

The following years were to witness the growing struggle between Argyll and Montrose, who, brought up in a tradition of honour and loyalty to his Sovereign's person, sided with the Royalists. There began that Campaign against Argyll and his followers which would lift Montrose's name to the highest honours of Scottish history. As a general, leader of men and inspiration to all who encountered him, the great Marquess, the most modest and devout of men, followed in the finest tradition of his nation's heroes. North of Perth he took command of a force of Highlanders and Irish from Antrim. A remarkable association was formed with Alastair Macdonald of Colonsay (Coll 'ciotach, meaning 'left handed'), the soldier marquess, finding an affinity with the Highland giant. With 1600 men, they swept the Highlands in victory after victory culminating in Argyll's humiliation in his own

*A magnificent Van Dyck portrait of King Charles I disguising his small stature.*

lands at Inverlochy. There followed the surrender of Glasgow and Edinburgh, but in using the savage Highlanders for his purposes, Montrose had both terrified and alienated many of his countrymen who might otherwise have supported him. His mobilisation of the Highland clans with their passionate support of their king as the chief of chiefs was a foretaste of what would follow thirty-seven years later.

The King was defeated at Naseby and the Scottish Covenanting army, still convinced that it could reform England to the oaths of Presbyterian thinking, returned. At the Battle of Philiphaugh, near Selkirk in September 1645, Montrose was routed by David Leslie, later Lord Newark. And it was to this Scottish army that King Charles surrendered in 1646, still obsessed with the divine right of kings and confident that the Scots would not hand him over to the English. Had he been less arrogant with them, been prepared to make some sort of deal concerning the £30,000 promised but not forthcoming from the Parliamentarians, he might have averted his personal disaster. One condition forced upon him at this point, was that Montrose should immediately disband and leave Scotland. His King's command to this effect left the loyal Montrose no option but to obey.

Charles I was handed over to the English Parliament, led by Oliver Cromwell. On 30th January 1649, he was executed at Whitehall. News of his death placed Scotland in a state of shock. Despite one of the bloodiest histories in Europe, Scotland had never had to resort to the formal and illegal execution of its Ard Righ. To rebel against a King was excusable; this conspired against all precedent, and as the message sank into the hearts of the Scottish people, they rallied to the cause of Charles' son, an exile in France.

At his father's request, Charles II had left the country aged 16. He had been devoted to his father, but was entirely different by nature. A dark, swarthy and sensual man, he was imbued with the Stewart's great talent to charm, an ability which he exploited to the full. Like his grandfather, he was cunning, undoubtedly an irrepressible opportunist, and ruthlessly prepared to sacrifice principle to gain his own ends.

And to begin with he was able to play with deep-felt shock and indignation felt by so many Scots at the manner of his father's death. Although aware of the bitter enmity between Argyll and Montrose, Charles II immediately set about recruiting both to his cause. Argyll was persuaded to proclaim the new King in Edinburgh, while Montrose, with 1,000 royalist Orcadians and 500 Danes, landed in Orkney. But Argyll had scores to settle with his great adversary. Montrose used the Castle of Dunbeath in Sutherland as the base for his forces, and shortly after, an ill-advised battle was fought at Carbisdale, where Montrose's forces were scattered and forced to flee across the River Oykell. Montrose himself fled to Ardvreck Castle in Assynt, home of Neil Macleod of Assynt, who treacherously handed him over to Argyll.

It could be supposed that Charles was truly powerless to save him. The King was intent on consolidating Argyll's support and certainly aware that Montrose's trial and execution for treason in May 1649 was the climax of an intensely personal feud. Yet Montrose's dignity on the scaffold was equal only to that of Charles I faced with the same fate. The crowd in the streets of Edinburgh, hired by Argyll to jeer as the noble Marquess was transported to his death, fell silent and many wept. Even the stirrings of the Clergy failed to provoke the required response. There is no doubt that Montrose's spirit, loyal to the end to a King who might have somehow extricated him from his fate, was a profound example to a people uncertain about their future.

In 1650, Charles II came to Scotland, agreed to the demands of the Covenanters and on 1st January 1651 was crowned King of Scots at Scone and it was Argyll himself who placed the Crown on his head. Cromwell's forces were already invading Scotland.

One can perhaps sidetrack at this point to consider the fate of the Scottish Regalia. At Scone, Charles II was to be the last British king to be crowned with the ancient Scottish crown. With Cromwell's forces advancing, it was considered adviseable to remove the various items — the Crown, Sceptre and Sword of State — out of harm's reach. The Covenanting party considered that rugged Dunnottar Castle on the Kincardineshire clifftops was as safe a location as any. Cromwell, incensed at Scotland's support for the King, was determined to capture them and melt them down as a gesture of contempt towards the Scottish policy.

The Governor of the Castle, George Ogilvie of Barras took possession of the Regalia, but word somehow leaked out and the Castle put under siege. As it was obvious that the Castle could not withstand an indefinite siege, plans were hatched to smuggle the Honours out.

Now the Governor's wife was friendly with Mrs Christian Granger, wife of the Rev. James Granger, minister of the neighbouring parish church of Kinneff. It was arranged that the Grangers' servant-girl should go frequently to the cliffs beneath the castle "on pretence of gathering dulse and tangles". Her visits became so regular that the Cromwellian troops began to pay no attention to her.

Finally, one day, the Honours were lowered over the cliff to the servant-girl and she packed them into her basket and covered them with seaweed. As the sword did not fit into the basket, it had been necessary to snap it in two. With her priceless burden, the girl walked calmly back along the cliffs in full sight of the enemy troops unchallenged.

The Regalia's first hiding place is reputed to have been at the bottom of the Minister's bed in the Manse. After a while, the items were transferred to the church, and on 31st March 1652, the Rev Granger wrote an account of their concealment to the Countess Marischall, so that at least somebody should know of their whereabouts should something befall himself. He reported that during the night he had dug a hole below the stone in front of the pulpit. There, he concealed the Crown and Sceptre. The sword he buried at the west end of the church, between two pews.

In June 1652, Ogilvie surrendered Dunnottar. He and his wife were called upon to surrender the Regalia, and failing to do so were imprisoned and cruelly treated. Neither revealed the secret of the Regalia's disappearance. After the Cromwell menace was over, and Charles restored, the Honours were retrieved and taken back to Edinburgh Castle, but with the King once more secure on the Throne of England, the Honours of Scotland took on a lesser relevance. Ensconced on the Throne of Scotland, Charles II had invaded England, but was soundly defeated at Worcester. He spent the following nine years in exile, and Cromwell's Treaty of Union between England and Scotland imposed an efficient military government which was extremely costly and universally detested. When Cromwell died and Charles II returned there was joyous reaction throughout the land.

It is probable that Charles' subsequent attitude towards his northern kingdom had been initiated by his dealings with the Covenanters. Certainly, he was to prove himself as two faced as many of them had been in dealing with him. He had, in fact, not the slightest intention of abiding by any agreements he had made to their cause, and, as it transpired, he never set foot in Scotland again. He saw to it, however, that action was taken on a number of fronts, particularly with regard to Argyll, who, having crowned him at Scone, had then made peace with Cromwell. This master of playing two sides off against one another met his just deserts from the executioner in 1661.

*Dunnottar Castle on the Kincardineshire clifftops, where the Scottish Regalia were taken for safety during Cromwell's invasion.*

But Charles was not a vengeful man, nor was he simply the frivolous, merry monarch which history leads us to believe. After the severity of puritan rule, England exploded into an orgy of self-indulgence which had a certain impact on the North, but the actual governance of Scotland was to be by the King's pen and through his Privy Council dominated by his agent, John Maitland, created Earl, later Duke of Lauderdale. Charles II was to prove himself a formidably resolute monarch, his parliament declaring that every act of Parliament from 1633 was to be considered invalid. It was Charles' clear intention to reinstate the power of the monarchy to what it had been in the days of his grandfather. Despite all his previous concessions towards the Covenanters, he had no intention of moving at all in their direction. It was as if his previous dealings with Scotland had left him with an attitude of contempt towards its peers.

In England the full episcopal concept was restored. From Scotland, James Sharp and Robert Leighton, representing the church, were despatched to London to see the King. Sharp returned as Archbishop of St Andrews and Primate of Scotland. Leighton was made Bishop of Dunblane. The former became so unpopular that his assassination by Covenanters in 1679 was generally regarded with approval.

As unrest continued, the government required that strong action be taken. A force commanded by John Graham of Claverhouse, who, like his great kinsman, Montrose, was possessed of a passionate loyalty towards his sovereign, inflicted savage reprisals until defeated at Drumclog, Lanarkshire. Charles immediately sent his natural son, the Duke of Monmouth to restore order. Monmouth, by virtue of his marriage to Anne Scott, younger daughter of Francis, 2nd Earl of Buccleuch, and his heiress, was a Scottish landowner himself. He wasted little time in suppressing the Covenanters at Bothwell Bridge, whereupon 1,200 prisoners were kept in outdoor confinement in Greyfriars Churchyard, not far from the Palace of Holyrood. About 800 took an oath of submission to secure their release, but many died, were executed or transported to slavery in the West Indies. This period became known as "The Killing Time" and did little to enhance Charles' reputation, and underlined that either the King had become distressingly unaware of the will of his Scottish subjects, or simply did not care. His brother James, Duke of York succeeded Lauderdale as Commissioner in 1679, but it was his personal Catholic zeal, not his lack of opportunity to understand, which removed this future king from the populus.

In England, the Whigs had sought to exclude James from the succession because of his religion. He had been married to Anne Hyde, daughter of Edward Hyde, Earl of Clarendon, Lord Chancellor of England. Many had considered her an unsuitable bride as she was not of royal or aristocratic blood, but she had earned popularity and bore James two daughters, Mary and Anne, both of whom were brought up in the Protestant faith. She had died in 1671, a convert to Catholicism and two years later James had remarried and to a fourteen-year-old Italian Princess, Mary of Modena, also a Catholic. The beautiful new Duchess of York exercised a strong influence on her husband's conversion, but it is obvious that the decision had already been taken.

The situation could have been so very different if Charles had fathered a legitimate heir. Sadly, while begetting a number of illegitimate offspring, his Portuguese Queen, Catherine de Braganza, remained barren. Now it is possible that a period of rule by a Catholic king might have been tolerated in the knowledge that his heirs were being brought up to be Protestant. But three years after Charles' death and his brother's succession, the Queen gave birth to a son.

Charles himself, had died a Catholic, having been received into that Church on his deathbed. James, openly subscribing to that religion, was inevitably watched with suspicion. And it is surprising that he was not more cautious about it. When Anglican friends pressed for him to return to the Established Church, he replied: "Never say anything to me again of turning Protestant. Do not expect it or flatter yourself that I shall ever be it; I never shall; and if occasion were, I hope God would give me grace to suffer death for the true religion . . ."

Charles' former commissioner, the Duke of Lauderdale, had written of James: "He is as very a papist as the Pope himself, which will be his ruin." If King James VII and II had been prepared to keep his religion to himself, his destiny might have been otherwise, but he seemed determined to establish a Catholic ascendancy. His brother, like their grandfather, had been more canny. Charles had once observed of his brother, "If James ever becomes King, he will never be able to hold it out four years to an end."

And Charles, forseeing perhaps the inevitable difficulties had arranged for his two nieces, at least, to be moulded and secured in the paths of Protestantism. It was arranged also that the eldest, Mary, should marry her cousin, the Protestant Prince William of Orange, Stadtholder of Holland, the only son of her aunt. Mary's sister Anne, lacked her sister's charm; indeed, was plump with an acid tongue. Both ladies had a tendency towards having false pregnancies in their marriages, and both cultivated intimate friendships with ladies around their own age, the former, as a teenager with a certain Mistress Cornwallis, and later with Sarah Jennings, the latter, primarily with Sarah Jennings, who had married John Churchill, later Duke of Marlborough. In July 1683, Anne married Prince George of Denmark, an uninspiring man with a liking for alcohol, but most suitably, a Protestant. "I have tried him drunk and I have tried him sober," remarked King Charles II, "but there is nothing in him." But Prince George did succeed over Dutch William by fathering a son. Alas, the young Prince died at the age of eleven.

The first threat to King James' throne came, however, from his brother's child by Lucy Walter. The Duke of Monmouth, created also Duke of Buccleuch at the age of twelve when he married the Buccleuch heiress, was held in great esteem by the people. Lucy Walter had always insisted that Charles had married her, and this Charles had never denied. On his restoration he had recognised Monmouth as illegitimate by creating him Duke, and Charles adored his swashbuckling, handsome and capable son, but not enough obviously to officially recognise him as his heir. Monmouth, encouraged by certain influential Whigs, devoutly desired that his father should do so.

As a Protestant, there was little doubt that he would be a deal more acceptable than his uncle. But his father remained adamant. Although Monmouth was appointed Captain General of the English Army, towards the end of his reign Charles issued a declaration that "on the word of a King and Faith of a Christian", he had married none other than Queen Catherine. It is said that years later a document of marriage was discovered by the then Duke of Buccleuch, but fearing the threat to the monarchy, the certificate was destroyed.

In June 1685, the Duke of Monmouth landed in the West Country and had himself proclaimed King at Taunton, in Somerset. In Scotland, the Earl of Argyll raised a force in his support, but Monmouth was badly let down by many who had promised to help. His rebellion was a complete failure and he was captured, imprisoned in the Tower and executed on St. Swithin's Day. In February 1687, James imposed a decree of religious toleration to both Catholics and Quakers, and then, to counteract the unpopularity of these measures, he granted toleration of the Presbyterian faith. Surprisingly, this failed to impress anybody; the threat of Popery remained, although many who had taken refuge in Holland began to return. The birth of a Catholic heir to the throne precipitated action.

On 5th November 1688, William of Orange invaded. In the 'Glorious Revolution' which followed, which in effect could not have been less glorious, son-in-law and nephew drove father-in-law and uncle out of his country. Prince George and Princess Anne disappeared from the Court at Whitehall. "God help me!" exclaimed James. "My own children have forsaken me!"

William, it appeared, had little desire to confront James and the advance towards London was improbably slow. It was as if he wanted James to evacuate the city on his own volition, and this is exactly what he did do. When William eventually arrived in London, the King and his Court had departed to France, where, as guests of King Louis XIV, a Court was set up at St. Germain-en-Leys, and the vanquished King James VII and II was to remain there for the rest of his life.

*John Knox, father of Scotland's Protestant revolution. His influence would linger for centuries after his death.*

# The Legacy of Glencoe

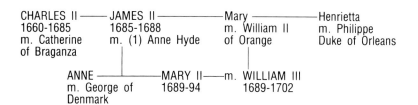

CHARLES II ——— JAMES II ————————— Mary ——————— Henrietta
1660-1685      1685-1688                    m. William II    m. Philippe
m. Catherine   m. (1) Anne Hyde            of Orange        Duke of Orleans
of Braganza

            ANNE ——————————MARY II——m. WILLIAM III
            m. George of        1689-94       1689-1702
            Denmark

# 9

## The Legacy of Glencoe

JAMES VII and II had barely set foot on French soil before a section of his subjects began to press for his return. Catholics and Episcopalians alike formed a 'Jacobite' movement to resist the new King William. In Scotland, the House of Stuart meant a great deal to ordinary folk, and particularly to Highlanders, many of whom were Catholic.

Although William III and Mary II became joint sovereigns on 11th April 1689, supplanting a rightful monarch, resistance was passive with only a few examples of force. The Duke of Gordon endeavoured to hold Edinburgh Castle in King James' name, but surrendered in June. The legendary Graham of Claverhouse, Viscount Dundee as he had become, raised a force of Highlanders and won a significant victory at the Pass of Killiecrankie in July. English troops commanded by General Mackay, had emerged at the upper end of the pass and had formed up facing north on the plateau above the Haugh of Urrard when the Highlanders were instructed to charge. Macaulay described what ensued as follows: "The Highlanders dropped their plaids. The few who were so luxurious as to wear rude socks of untanned hide spurned them away. It was long remembered in Lochaber that Lochiel took off what possibly was the only pair of shoes in his clan, and charged barefoot at the head of his men. In two minutes, the battle was lost and won . . ." Although the Highlanders won the battle, Dundee himself was slain, a blow from which the Jacobite forces were never to recover. Without his leadership, their morale disintegrated, and three weeks later they were soundly defeated at Dunkeld. Such forces as remained, were wiped out at Cromdale the following year. As a symbol of victory, and as a base from which to control the Highlands, King William built Fort William on the West Coast. He further demanded an oath of allegiance from the Highland chiefs, to be sworn by 1st January 1692.

It had obviously been decided that a lesson should be made of the Highlands, but the exiled king kept close contact with his Highlanders, realising that they remained his principle hope of support, and James grasped the futility of their situation. He instantly instructed that they should take the oath, and thereby certainly averted a major massacre. The time was not right; the Jacobites must bide their time. But what followed although admittedly a small affair, was one which, through its implications of treachery and dishonour, was to sour the Highlands for ever against the usurpers of the Jacobite throne.

Exactly who devised the plan will probably never be discovered, but it is certain that Sir John Dalrymple, Master of Stair, who had become joint Secretary of State for Scotland, was heavily implicated. It was widely understood that the Highlands were Jacobite in sympathy; in order to emphasise the strength of the new establishment, it was felt that a strong gesture must be made. As fate would have it, destiny singled out a remote, ill-prepared and luckless little community in Glencoe.

A senior member of Clan Campbell was heard to comment that he could not understand what all the fuss was about when it had been such a piffling little incident, when only some 32 tinkers, cattle rustlers and miscreants were seen off into the hills. This might well have been the attitude of many Lowlanders who heard of the business at the time, but there were matters far more fundamental involved; the callous abuse of hospitality, but more serious, the cold blooded initiation of murder by a government and King who in the South of England were obsessed with human rights and civilised behaviour.

The MacIan MacDonalds of Glencoe were poor, Catholic and had a history of disorder against their powerful Campbell neighbours. Their chief was elderly and that winter the snows had been hard. He set off to swear his oath at Fort William, but on arrival discovered that he would have to go to Inveraray on the side of Loch Fyne. As a result, he was late in his supplication, and when the papers arrived in Edinburgh a few days later, they

*King James VII & II as Duke of York by Lely, and before he was driven from his throne by his daughter and son-in-law.*

DVKE OF YORK

were suppressed by Stair, who seeing the opportunity for an example, issued "letters of fire and sword".

The massacre took place at dawn on 13th February 1692. The order for it is said to have been written on the nine of diamonds, since then known as the "curse of Scotland". There were 200 occupants in the glen and forty were slain. Others escaped, but many died of exposure. Although three years later a Scottish Parliament voted that the killing had been murder, there were no reprisals. The main instigators, Stair, Robert Campbell of Glenlyon and the Earl of Breadalbane were loudly condemned, but went free. King William was in Holland at the time and undoubtedly regarded the episode with little interest, well warranting Andrew Fletcher of Saltoun's comment that "Scotland is a farm managed by servants and not under the eye of the master".

Scotland entered a period of malaise with a serious famine occuring in the 1690s. Another major cause of discontent was an enterprise of a commercial nature in which many Scots placed their savings. The economist William Paterson won support for the establishment of a colony on the isthmus of Darien in South America. An expedition of 1,200 settlers took part in the project, but after a year the colony was abandoned, defeated by tropical disease and the hostility of English and Spanish alike. A second attempt was mounted, but failed. The Darien fiasco caused financial ruin to many Scots and although King William was probably little acquainted with the business, this did not prevent many from holding him and his government responsible.

Queen Mary died of smallpox in 1694 and King William eight years later. Neither were greatly mourned in Scotland.

But to his credit, or otherwise, depending upon differing points of view, William, before his death, had spoken strongly in favour of a formal union between Scotland and England. There were very obvious difficulties in having two legislatures with much common debate, and there were other factors to be taken into consideration.

The new Queen Anne was heartbroken at the death of her only son, William, Duke of Gloucester, from dropsy. Her false pregnancies became the object of some derision, and it was certain that she would not succeed in producing a second heir. At the same time a Catholic Jacobite heir was growing up in France. Some Protestant provision for the future must be made.

*Glen Coe, in Argyllshire. The notorious massacre of 1692, a betrayal of Highland hospitality, would never be forgotten.*

With the Act of Settlement, parliament decreed that the British Crown should bypass forty-two Catholic heirs in favour of the nearest Protestant candidate, and that person was Sophia, daughter of James VI's daughter Elizabeth, who had married Frederick, Elector of Palatine and for a brief, romantic time had reigned as the "Winter Queen" of Bohemia, before the forces of European Catholicism had driven her and her husband into exile in the Hague. It had been their third son, the dashing Rupert of the Rhine, who had rallied to his Uncle, Charles I's aid and proved such a dazzling general on his behalf. Sophia had married the Elector of Hanover, and, it transpired, was to be mother of the first Hanovarian King of England and Scotland.

The Act of Union 1707 created Great Britain. Scotland was no longer legally a separate nation, and consequently many Scots bitterly resented this legislation. But now Scotland was to send 45 members of parliament to the the re-formed Parliament at Westminster. A number of other developments transpired; Scotland was allowed equal trading rights at home and overseas, and English customs and excise laws were exercised in Scotland. The legal structure, however, remained the same.

In 1713, the Scots decided that they did not like the Act, and a motion in the House of Lords to dissolve the Union was defeated by only four votes. It was felt that the people of Scotland had had Union forced upon them by their peers who sought self-advancement in the land. It was felt that had the people of Scotland been consulted on the subject, they would never have accepted it.

Thus the monarchy of Scotland was merged into that of England and Wales. James V's words that it "passed with a lass", therefore, proved prophetic not about his daughter Mary, but concerned his great-great-great granddaughter Queen Anne. Her successor was James V's great-great-great grandson, George of Hanover.

But there had been signs towards the end of Anne's reign that she was becoming reconciled to her father's son. Various Jacobite appointments excited comment. It was known that her officers, Oxford and Bolingbroke, were in communication with the Jacobites, and Anne had expressed concern when a price had been placed on her step-brother's head in 1708.

In 1714, Prince James wrote to Anne urging that measures be taken to secure his succession, and promising that as a condition of his recognition, he would take no steps to overthrow his step-sister's government. A report was circulated in Holland at a later date claiming that Anne had been negotiating a reconciliation for him. The Whig government's declaration that a member of the electoral family of Hanover should visit London had infuriated the Queen, and when a writ of summons for the electoral prince as Duke of Cambridge was obtained, Anne forbade the Hanovarian envoy her presence, naming all who supported the project, her enemies.

This then was the situation when Queen Anne died on 1st August 1714. The restoration of a Stuart monarch might well have been achieved had she lived longer as there was widespread feeling in the country against the Government's choice. And particularly in Scotland where the absence of a monarch created myths; and where general dissatisfaction against Westminster government was deep felt. The Scots still retained a nostalgic affection for the Stuarts, and in their absence, the desire to identify with absent kings increased.

King George I was born in 1660, heir, through his father Ernest Augustus to the hereditary lay Bisphopric of Osnabruck, and to the duchy of Calenberg, which formed one portion of the Hanovarian possessions of the house of Brunswick, whilst he secured the reversion of the other portion, the duchy of Celle by his marriage with his heiress cousin, Sophia Dorothea. The marriage was not a success. The prince acquired mistresses, and, indeed, ones who lacked both beauty and intelligence. His wife, not surprisingly, found a lover, and being discovered, was divorced in 1694. Infidelity was considered the privilege of the male in Hanovarian society. When their great-grandson King George IV attempted to divorce his wife in England for similar promiscuity, he was soundly criticised.

King George I arrived in England unable to speak the language, anxious to use his new found position to obtain advantages for his German principality, and inclined to indulge his retinue of German attendants and mistresses to their financial betterment. He disliked the English, and they, in turn, were not impressed. Had his cousin James in France, the "King over the Water" been of a stronger mould and had his supporters been more honourable, then the Stuarts could easily have returned at this juncture. But the Jacobite cause was to be fought and lost in the Scottish Highlands.

# The Kings over the water

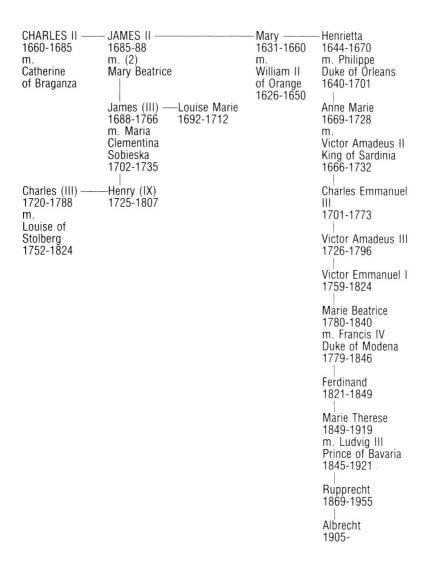

CHARLES II ——— JAMES II ——————————————— Mary ——— Henrietta
1660-1685      1685-88                                 1631-1660   1644-1670
m.             m. (2)                                   m.          m. Philippe
Catherine      Mary Beatrice                            William II  Duke of Orleans
of Braganza                                             of Orange   1640-1701
                                                        1626-1650

               James (III) ——Louise Marie                          Anne Marie
               1688-1766      1692-1712                             1669-1728
               m. Maria                                             m.
               Clementina                                          Victor Amadeus II
               Sobieska                                            King of Sardinia
               1702-1735                                           1666-1732

Charles (III) ———Henry (IX)                                        Charles Emmanuel
1720-1788        1725-1807                                         III
m.                                                                 1701-1773
Louise of
Stolberg                                                          Victor Amadeus III
1752-1824                                                          1726-1796

                                                                  Victor Emmanuel I
                                                                  1759-1824

                                                                  Marie Beatrice
                                                                  1780-1840
                                                                  m. Francis IV
                                                                  Duke of Modena
                                                                  1779-1846

                                                                  Ferdinand
                                                                  1821-1849

                                                                  Marie Therese
                                                                  1849-1919
                                                                  m. Ludvig III
                                                                  Prince of Bavaria
                                                                  1845-1921

                                                                  Rupprecht
                                                                  1869-1955

                                                                  Albrecht
                                                                  1905-

# 10

## The Kings over the Water

IN France, the Jacobite Court existed under the patronage of the "Sun King", Louis XIV. An ardent Catholic, he had no doubts as to who the King of England, Scotland and Ireland should be, and he saw that person's role as highly beneficial in influencing the political games of Europe at that time. But an ill-conceived attempt at invasion, landing in Southern Ireland in 1689, proved a dismal failure.

At the Chateau of St Germain in 1707, on his father's death, a thirteen year old boy, also James, was proclaimed King of England and Scotland. It was reminiscent of the boy's Stewart ancestors who had also inherited at an early age but, unlike them, he was dominated by no Regent other than his widowed mother, a devout and determined woman who nevertheless was happy to see her son grow to maturity in the lavish circles of the French Court. But then he was without a kingdom, and the occasion of Queen Anne's death meant only that the twenty year old claimant to her throne must be seen to act.

His natural brother, the Duke of Berwick, a notable soldier in European disputes, had other ideas. "To believe that with the Scots alone he will succeed in his enterprise has always been regarded by me as madness," was his comment on the subject. The Duke, a resolute campaigner, was realistic, but James as the heir to the Stuart throne was far too deeply committed not to grasp at any opportunity which presented itself. And throughout Britain it was reported that his interests were being widely acclaimed.

On a September day in 1715, the Earl of Mar raised the blue and gold Stuart banner at Braemar, proclaiming "the Chevalier

*The "Old Pretender", James VIII by Francis de Troy, as a young man in exile in France.*

of St. George; our right and natural King James VIII, by the Grace of God, who is now coming to relieve us from our oppressions". Detached by distance and thought from the centres of government, Edinburgh and London, if the former could still be identified as such, all Scotland north of the River Tay responded. As fate would have it, the Scottish uprising was not supported by the expected insurrections in the North and South-West of England. It had been intended that James would land on the south coast, but the ringleaders panicked at the last moment and fled to France.

The Earl of Mar rallied 5,000 men — Scottish nobles, chieftains and their Highlanders and marched on Edinburgh. An attempt to seize the castle failed and the army rested at Perth. In the meantime, the Duke of Argyll, who had gathered up the government supporters, marched to Stirling, and here, within forty miles of the Jacobites, he waited.

At Preston, on 14th November 1715, Jacobite forces led by Lord Derwentwater with some Scots led by Lord Kenmure, were defeated and their leaders executed. The day before, Argyll had coaxed Mar into a confrontation at Sheriffmuir, near Stirling, and the battle which ensued had been so inconclusive that both sides had claimed it as a victory.

Encouraged by the news of a Jacobite victory, James had set out to Scotland. Mar, meantime, had panicked and fled north. Two days before Christmas, James landed at Peterhead, in poor health having only recently recovered from measles. There was nobody to meet him. Forty-four days later he was to depart from Montrose leaving behind a desolate country and a demoralised people. Sadly, James was no leader of men, failing entirely to inspire the Jacobite force which at one point had swollen to 12,000 in number, but who, as Argyll's army approached, melted into the winter snows.

James left behind him a letter to the Duke of Argyll. He assured him that he had regretted giving the order for a "scorched earth" policy during his retreat. James would ensure that compensation was raised for those who had suffered. The Hanovarians, however, had no such humanitarian sentiments. The people of the Highlands bore the full wrath of their southern rulers. One contemporary report to James in France speaks of "Nothing but an entire desolation from Stirling to Inverness." James himself wrote sadly of the venture that he would have thought himself to some degree content had he been alone in his misfortune. But the nature of the Highlands had always been to rise against oppression and, in its way, the ruthless severity of the measures to be enforced upon a proud people was to kindle a bitter flame that thirty years later would turn once again to fire.

But for James it was over. Seized with a singular melancholy over his failure, he became increasingly introspective. And the "Old Pretender" discovered that nobody in Europe particularly wanted to be associated with him. King Louis XIV of France, his father's champion who on James VII and II's deathbed had taken his farewell of him with the words, "Adieu, mon frère, le meilleur, le plus outragé des hommes" (Farewell, my brother, the best and most wronged of men), had died. Politics in Europe were ever volatile and the "Old Pretender" was no longer the great hope of Catholicism, but an embarrassment. France, ruled by a Regent, had no desire to harbour such a person, and the only welcoming voice, it transpired, was that of the Vatican. This faced James with a serious dilemma. By taking protection from the Pope, James would certainly alienate his Protestant supporters in Britain. And so it was that James began his travels. To begin with, he went to the Papal town of Avignon, but the British Government put pressure of the Vatican, not wishing to see a settlement of Jacobites building up strength in that corner of France. Compliant with the situation, rather than being forced to move on, James travelled to Turin, where his cousin, the Queen of Sardinia, made him welcome. From there he moved to his great uncle's Palace at Modena, and here, he fell in love with his cousin, Princess Benedicta, a match which was promptly vetoed by her father. So, exasperated, James moved on at last to Rome, and here a marriage was arranged with Princess Maria Clementina Sobieska, youngest daughter to Prince James Sobieski, pretender to the Polish throne.

The Sobieskis were connected with the ruling houses of Spain, Austria and Bavaria, and were wealthy. The idea of such a match had little appeal for King George I of Britain, who did his utmost to prevent it, including arranging for the bridal party to be arrested in Austria and held prisoners for six months in a castle at Innsbruck.

The story of Clementina's escape from the Schloss Ambras is in the best traditions of Stuart drama. A dedicated Irish Jacobite, Captain Charles Wogan conceived a daring escape plan, and, collaborating with a castle maid, stole a key and Clementina was able to leave the Schloss leaving the maid in her place. They then embarked upon a 200 mile dash to the frontier between the Empire and the Papal States, all the time hotly pursued. When, at last, Clementina arrived safely at her destination, she discovered that her husband-to-be, possibly jolted from his malaise by his impending marriage, had departed to Spain to raise support for his cause.

At Bologna on 9th May 1719, Clementina was married to James by proxy. At Rome, a splendid apartment had been prepared for her, but it was to be four months before she was to set eyes on her husband for the first time. At Montefiascone, 70 miles from Rome, a second marriage ceremony took place, and it was generally agreed by all that they made an attractive couple. From then on, the Palazzo Muti in Rome became the centre of the Jacobite cause, and however the rest of Europe might have

*The marriage of James VIII to Clementina Sobieska in Rome by Masucci.*

regarded the newly-married couple, in Rome they were respect-
fully treated as King James III and Queen Maria Clementina.
Something of the esteem in which they were held can be gleaned
from the fact that when Clementina gave birth to her first child
on 31st December 1720, it was in the presence of over one
hundred cardinals, members of royal families, ambassadors and
other distinguished personages. In Rome there were great
celebrations, and France, once again, greeted the birth of a Stuart
heir with an unexpected rapture. The child was christened
Charles Edward and pronounced Prince of Wales.

Across the English Channel, George I's popularity had gone
steadily into decline from the moment he had landed. Despite
this, however, few were prepared to reject him in favour of a
Catholic replacement. George had elevated his two remarkably
unappealing mistresses and waged a constant feud with his son
and heir. But a Whig dominated government shrewdly administered by such statesmen as Robert Walpole kept the country
under control.

In Rome, in March 1725, a second son was born to the "Old
Pretender", and christened Henry Benedict, Duke of York. At
the same time, it became obvious that James and Clementina

*Above: James VIII's younger son, Prince Henry Benedict, destined to become a Cardinal of Rome. (Antonio David).*

*Left: Prince Charles Edward Stuart — the "Young Pretender". (Antonio David).*

were not getting on as well as they had been immediately after the wedding. Possibly the ambitious Clementina was disappointed with her role as *de jure* Queen, and no doubt she felt that her husband was doing little to remedy the situation. Rumours of their arguments began to spread and in November 1725, Clementina removed herself to a convent. Ten years later she died there, greatly mourned by her abandoned husband and her two sons.

The eldest of these two sons grew up to be something of a Prince Charming in the eyes of the European courts. His dark eyes, fair complexion and curly blonde hair coupled with a taste for elegant dressing made this self-styled Count of Albany something of an idol in the social circles of Italy and, later, in France.

By this time, King George II, a plump, unprepossessing figure had succeeded his father. His attitude to Britain he hardly took trouble to disguise. "The devil," he said, "can take the whole island, provided I can get out of it and go to Hanover". But at the same time he was known to boast that he had not one drop of blood in his veins that was not English. It transpires, however, that his Queen Caroline became the astute politician at court, cultivating Walpole, and it was Walpole, while Queen Caroline lived, who kept the Jacobites at bay.

Towards 1743, things began to change. Queen Caroline had died in 1737, and in 1740, England had gone to war with Spain. In 1742, Walpole resigned, and in 1743 Cardinal de Tencin, Louis XV of France's chief minister invited Prince Charles Edward Stuart to come to Paris. After some hesitation, James agreed that his son should go, at the same time issuing a declaration nominating, "Our dearest Son, Charles, Prince of Wales to be sole Regent of Our Kingdoms of England, Scotland and Ireland, and all Our other Dominions, during Our Absence".

Although Charles' reception in Paris could hardly be described as warm, Louis XV became increasingly interested in the proposed expedition, although keeping a personal distance from the Prince whom he viewed as conceited. A force of 7000 men under Marshal Saxe with a fleet of transportation was prepared to set sail from Dunkirk. But then a violent storm blew up causing damage to the French fleet in the Channel and almost destroying the transportation at Dunkirk. It was a bitter blow enhanced by the almost immediate departure of Marshal Saxe to fight in Flanders.

The effect on the young Charles could have been shattering, and it is true to say that for a period, he immersed himself in frivolity with a group of hot blooded young men notable for their irresponsibility. But to his credit, he did not lose sight of his objective, and although there were constant promises of aid from England, France and Scotland, it rapidly dawned on the Prince that he must act alone. He knew that his father would never sanction such action, but he became convinced that he must go to Scotland and start an uprising.

On 5th July 1745, two ships set sail from Brittany. On board were the Prince, the Duke of Atholl, Francis Strickland, George Kelly, Aeneas Macdonald, John O'Sullivan, Sir John Macdonnell and Sir Thomas Sheridan. His companions were to be recorded in history as the "Seven Men of Moidart". The Prince wrote to

*Glenfinnan at the head of Loch Shiel. In the foreground is the monument commemorating the 1745 rebellion.*

his father: "I have taken a firm resolution to conquer or dye, and stand my ground as long as I have a man remaining with me".

Eventually, the Prince's ship approached the Western Isles and, after a preliminary excursion onto Barra, the Prince landed on the Isle of Eriksay. The story goes that as he struggled against the wind to climb up a hill, a packet of seed collected in France fell from his pocket. To this day it is said that a rose-pink flower grows along this strip of Eriskay shoreline.

The welcome was not encouraging. The party found shelter in a poor, island croft, and the following morning, having returned to his ship, the *Du Teillay*, Charles received Alexander Macdonald of Boisdale, who had travelled from South Uist. Far from enthusing about the Prince's venture, Macdonald explained that he could do nothing to support Charles. Indeed, he advised the party to return home immediately.

"I am come home," responded the Prince.

At the head of Loch Shiel, twenty seven days later Prince Charles Edward Stuart, to be known as the "Young Pretender", demonstrated to one and all that he had meant what he had said. And he could hardly have chosen a more powerfully romantic setting than the shimmering loch, and Glenfinnan, with its impressive backdrop of mountains.

But there is no doubt that he must have been disappointed with the initial one hundred and fifty Macdonald clansmen who awaited him on his arrival. There was no other course but to wait himself, and some two hours later he was rewarded when seven hundred Highlanders came streaming down the glen. At the head came Donald Cameron of Locheil with his clansmen. Behind them came three hundred more Macdonalds. Without hesitation the Prince unfurled and raised his red and white banner.

That he had come this far can be attributed almost solely to the remarkable charm of this Jacobite prince. Although ridiculed by many then, and later, after his failure, there is every proof that Charles Edward Stuart possessed the qualities of leadership and the captivating manners of his ancestors. Like so many of his mould, it was to be the petty squabbles and failings of those about him which would bring him down. But at the time, all who saw him were profoundly impressed with his utter determination to follow his chosen course.

"If he succeeds," commented Lord Lovat, "the whole merit will be his own; and if his mad Enterprise bring misfortunes upon him, he has only himself to blame."

Without further hesitation Charles Edward Stuart marched on Edinburgh. The Government, startled, offered a reward of £30,000 for his capture, and Sir John Cope, in command of Government forces in Scotland, moved his army north. The two armies, however, passed each other by, Cope retiring for the moment to Inverness, and thus allowing his enemy a major psychological victory which rallied hundreds to the cause.

By the time the Jacobites reached Perth, Prince Charles Edward had gained the support of the Duke of Perth, Lord George Murray, Lord Ogilvy, Lord Nairn, Lord Strathallan, Macpherson of Cluny, Oliphant of Gask and others. With over 2,500 men, Bonnie Prince Charlie pressed on south. On 17th September 1745 he entered his Capital.

The refined inhabitants of Edinburgh certainly had mixed feelings about the coming of the Highland hordes. But once again, the Prince's charm and elegance entirely captivated his citizens. He wore Highland dress and a blue velvet bonnet. His Star of the Order of St Andrew and his silver hilted sword shone in the sunlight. All who caught sight of him gasped at his dazzling good looks, and remember that it was many years since Scotland had seen their Royal Family.

Although a Government force occupied Edinburgh Castle, the Prince took up residence at Holyrood Palace. At Market Cross, a crowd comprising a cross section of Edinburgh worthies, witnessed the proclaiming of James III of England and James VIII of Scotland. But so far, the going had been too easy. From Aberdeen, Sir John Cope's forces sailed to Dunbar and on the 21st September Bonnie Prince Charlie experienced his first taste of victory at the Battle of Prestonpans, a confrontation which lasted ten minutes before the terrified government soldiers fled before the wild Highland onslaught.

When the Prince returned to Edinburgh that day, his welcome was tumultuous. Overnight, everybody in Scotland had turned Jacobite.

The Prince still had hopes of French back-up support, although he was anxious to exploit his success and march on the South. Reports came through that Marshall Wade had arrived at Newcastle, and that reinforcements were on their way to join his army. There was no time to delay, and in November, the Jacobite army, now numbering 8,000 was on the move. Although his progress over the Border attracted few recruits, there was an air of confidence about the Prince's action, although others had their doubts. And it is true to say that there were many who pressed the king to remain in Edinburgh, reject the Act of Union and claim Scotland as his realm. It is interesting to speculate on the way of things had he taken this course. But it became apparent over this period that the Prince and his senior Lieutenant, Lord George Murray, a son of the 1st Duke of Atholl, were not seeing eye to eye. Although a man of distinctive military talents, Lord George was an opinionated and tactless person, but who carried nevertheless the support of the other chiefs who bowed to the wisdom of his age and experience against that of the impetuous Prince.

The Prince's army reached Derby on 4th December. In London King George II was preparing to leave for Hanover while his son, the Duke of Cumberland was frenzied in an attempt to raise a second army. Had the Prince's followers pressed home the advantage and marched on London, who knows what the outcome could have been. Instead, they lost their nerve. The Prince knew that to retreat would be taken as an admission of failure. After all, he had come so far through sheer unmitigated daring. Furthermore, his Highlanders were stirred up for a fight. But Lord George and his cronies prevailed. It is probably true to say that by taking this course, the Jacobites threw away any hope of success thereafter.

The disappointed army returned to Scotland, although the Prince seemed to be doing all he could to delay its progress, determined that it should not look as if they were running away. They were back in Scotland before Christmas Day, but the climate of events was rapidly changing. Government troops had retaken Edinburgh and some of the clans hitherto neutral came out against the Prince. The relationship between him and Lord George had deteriorated still further when the Prince decided to lay siege to Stirling Castle. Nevertheless, the Prince was adamant, and with fresh troops under Lord John Drummond and Lord Strathallan, this was put into effect.

But the freezing winds and rain had taken their toll, and it was hardly surprising after his various ordeals that the Prince should be taken ill. At Bannockburn, he rested and was nursed by his host's niece, Clementina Walkinshaw. That the Prince should be attracted to this plain girl in her mid-thirties is a surprise, being totally out-of-character, but then love moves in a mysterious way, so they say. Having had the pick of the beauties at Holyrood, it was unexpected that he should fall for Clementina, but perhaps it was that he did not feel threatened by her. He made her promise to come to him should he need her.

The Prince recovered from his influenza to hear that General George Hawley was advancing on the Jacobites at Stirling. On 17th January 1746, the two armies met at Falkirk. Whereas the Battle of Prestonpans had taken ten minutes, the Battle of Falkirk took twenty. Again the Government forces were terrified by the Highland foot-soldiers and fled before them. But it was a short lived victory. Stirling Castle refused to yield, and the Prince was pursuaded to give up his efforts in this direction and fall back to Inverness, where he set up headquarters. At Aberdeen, meantime, the Duke of Cumberland was assembling his army.

The Battle of Culloden Moor which took place on 16th April 1746 was to have repercussions which Scotland would never forget. Five thousand Jacobites, ill-armed and hungry, faced a government force of 9,000. In the ensuing turmoil, only 76 of the government troops fell, while after the battle, the count of Highland dead reached 1,200. As the fighting lapsed, William Augustus, Duke of Cumberland was to truly earn his name of "The Butcher" by giving the order that no wounded should be spared.

On seeing the battle lost, the Prince's message to his commanders was that "every one should look out for the means of saving himself as best he can". In many ways it was to be regretted that the Prince himself did not fall at Culloden, for it might have saved his reputation from being blemished by the decline of a demoralised, defeated man. But as it transpired, the immediate next stage of the Prince's story was to take him into the realms of legend. While Scotland suffered the ravages of the Duke of Cumberland's revenge, while the British government took steps to systematically disband and destroy the Clan system which had opposed their King, Prince Charles Edward Stuart took to the heather.

The manhunt was on. A price of £30,000 was still placed on the Prince's head. In an attempt to find one of the several French ships despatched to save him, he fled first to the West Coast and to South Uist, and it was from here that he escaped to Skye and to an encounter which was to become immortalised as one of the great romantic partnerships of all time. In fact, the Prince's association with the 24-year old Flora Macdonald lasted little more than a week.

With the waters of the Hebrides thick with government ships, it was vital that the Prince should leave South Uist for Skye, but under the circumstances it seemed an almost impossible project. It so happened that staying with her brother at Milton, was Flora, who normally resided with her mother on Skye. The proposition put to her, and which she at first firmly rejected, was that the Prince should travel over the sea as her companion, "Betty Burke". Only on being confronted by the Prince himself, did Flora agree to the hazardous plan. In the event, clothes were stitched for the six-foot prince by Lady Clanranald, and on 28th June, the Young Pretender, in sprigged dress, white apron, frilly cap and cloak, set off in a boat with Flora rowed by five boatmen.

For no accountable reason, the boat was fired on by militia as it neared the shore at Waternish, so they were forced to land at another point. At Lady Macdonald's house, Flora encountered a Lieutenant from the militia who was searching for the Prince, but she managed to dispose of any suspicions he might have had. Lady Macdonald herself was far from calm, but a kinsman, her husband's factor came to their aid. Macdonald of Kingsburgh.

Kingsburgh discovered the Prince on a hillside hiding among a flock of sheep and invited him to come to his home. When his wife realised the identity of the extraordinary woman who had entered their home, she cried: "O Lord, we are a' ruined and undone for ever!" But he stayed the night with them, and the

*Flora Macdonald by Wilson — she was in the Prince's company for less than a week, yet their association became legendary.*

following morning set off for Portree where he found Flora waiting.

Late that night, he set sail for Raasay. "For all that has happened, Madam, I hope that we shall meet at St. James's yet," he had said to Flora as he took his leave. He had no means of rewarding her, so he gave her "Betty Burke's" blue velvet garters as a memento.

Flora's own destiny was itself a spirited one. On returning to her mother's home at Armadale she was arrested and taken to the Tower of London for imprisonment. In 1747, she was allowed to go free under the Act of Indemnity and three years later married Allen Macdonald of Kingsburgh with whom she emigrated to the Carolinas. Caught up in the American War of Independence, they journeyed to Nova Scotia, and in 1779 she returned to Skye in a merchant ship which was attacked by privateers. She refused to leave the deck during the action and was wounded in the arm as a result. This brave and courageous lady died in 1790.

Meantime, the Prince continued his flight. After two months on Raasay, he returned to Skye, and then to the mainland. It is said that for over three hundred miles he walked, ran and crawled over mountain and glen. Nobody betrayed him, although virtually every day he was on the point of being discovered. But while he moved around, his heart would have been burdened with the desolation he must have seen — ruined crops, burned out crofts and houses, the price of his failure. But the fact that their Prince was still free, was still at liberty in the hills, was a great inspiration to those who still believed in him. Barefoot and ragged in his adversity, he amazed his companions and those who saw him with his high spirits. In a schoolboyish way, he was heard to boast, "I live like a Prince".

On 6th September 1746, the privateers *L'Hereux* and *Le Prince de Conti*, anchored in Loch nam Uamh, north east from the Sound of Arisaig. A message found the Prince hiding on the slopes of Ben Alder in a shelter which became known as "The Cage", and a week later he was rowed out to *L'Hereux* from the shore by the light of the moon. As *L'Hereux* set sail the next morning, one can only imagine the Prince's thoughts as he watched his devastated country fade from sight across the grey seas.

But the Jacobite story did not end there, although it would not again directly involve the people of Scotland. In the almost contemptuous absence of their Hanovarian monarchs, the Scots pre-occupied themselves with their everyday lives, but there are to this day those who raise their glasses engraved with a white rose to drink the health of the "Kings across the Water".

The Young Pretender returned to France where he was joined by his brother, the Duke of York, at Fontainebleau as guests of Louis XV. The brothers were very different, and the young Duke disapproved of his brother's flamboyance. Family arguments in the best Hanovarian style began to take place, enhanced when Henry, Duke of York announced that he intended to take Holy Orders and enter the Church of Rome. In 1750, Prince Charles, who had by then begun his wanderings throughout Europe, slipped into London undetected for a brief visit. While there, he took the opportunity to be converted to the Anglican faith, which may indicate that he still had hopes of achieving his ultimate ambition. Then, in 1712, in the city of Ghent, he sent for Clementina Walkinshaw and the following year she gave birth to their daughter who was christened Charlotte. But they did not marry and this brought nothing but distress to his father and brother, who was on his way to becoming a Cardinal. Pressure was applied, but eventually it was Clementina who walked out on the Prince giving as reason his violent fits of temper. With Charlotte, she settled in a Convent in the Rue St Jacques, Paris.

In 1766, the Old Pretender died at the Palazzo Muti, Rome. His heir, who considered himself King Charles III of Great Britain, but often called himself the Count of Albany, was well on his way into obscurity when in 1770, the French Government suddenly took an interest in him and offered him a pension of 40,000 crowns to marry and produce an heir. It seemed that France liked to have a Stuart heir and ally waiting in the wings.

The bride they had found for the fifty year old Charles was a nineteen year old Princess, Louise Maximilienne Caroline Emmanuele of Stolberg, whose mother was descended from the House of Bruce. They were married by proxy in Paris and then she travelled to Rome to meet her husband where an official ceremony took place. The bride, it transpired, knew exactly what she was doing — with no dowry her future prospects were limited. The new "Queen" played her role brilliantly, holding receptions and salons, and soon attracted a large band of adoring followers. Charles began to drink heavily, unable to compete.

In 1774, the couple left Rome for Pisa. It is claimed that here Louise gave birth to a child, but this has never been substantiated. Later they moved to Florence, but Charles continued to drink and their life together became a misery. It is hardly surprising that Louise eventually left her husband for a handsome young poet named Vittorio Alfieri.

In 1788, the Young Pretender died in Rome. Forgotten by his contemporaries, ignored, cursed as a failure and a drunk, Charles Edward Stuart is nonetheless one of the most colourful and shining characters of Scotland's heritage. His body was first buried in the Cathedral of Frascati, above the vault where his cyprus-wood coffin was laid to rest is a memorial tablet surmounted by the British royal coat of arms in bronze. His Cardinal brother, who now became named Henry IX, King of Great Britain, officiated at the ceremony, and it was with the death of this "Cardinal King" in 1807, that the direct line of the Stuart succession ended. By then, the Vatican had allowed that the remains of James VIII and Charles III be interred at St Peter's, Rome. A white marble tomb carved by Canova commemorates

*Prince Charles Edward Stuart in old age by H. D. Hamilton — a disappointed, disillusioned man.*

the three claimant kings — "far from Scotland in body and spirit, but unforgotten."

Through searching back to King Charles I's daughter Henrietta, who had married Philippe, Duke of Orleans, and through her descendants' marriages into the Royal Houses of Savoy (Sardinia), the Estes of Modena and the Wittelsbachs of Bavaria, the Jacobites identify their present claimant as the Duke of Bavaria, although it seems improbable that the present title-holder would ever think to press such.

And in Scotland, while the sentiment lingered after Culloden, encouraged by the widespread unpopularity of the Hanovarians, it faded with the passage of time.

# 11

## Comings and Goings

IN the years after Culloden, the Scots did not have the opportunity to welcome their monarchs to Scotland. But there was
the occasional diversion, such as the arrival in 1796, of Charles
Philippe, Comte d'Artois, who landed at Leith from the Royal
Navy frigate *Jason*. The tables had turned and an heir presump-
tive to the throne of France sought refuge at the Court of a
British king.

The Count and his followers were installed at Holyrood, and
certainly their welcome was prestigious enough with a 21 gun
salute from Edinburgh Castle. But the Prince was desperately in
debt, and his brother King Louis XVI of France, and his sister-
in-law, Queen Marie Antoinette, seized by the Paris mob, would
no longer be able to bail him out.

And it was politic that King George III should take pity on
this fugitive member of what had been one of Europe's greatest
Royal houses. Furthermore, those in Scotland who had initially
supported the egalitarian concepts of the French Revolution, had
become disgusted by the subsequent Reign of Terror. Holyrood,
being obscurely designated a "debtor's sanctuary" suited the
Count well, and he was to use it as a base until the French
monarchy was eventually restored in 1814. Then, having succeeded to the throne on the death of his brother, King Louis
XVIII, as King Charles X, he found himself deposed in favour
of his sons, and then Louis Philippe. Once again, in 1830, he
returned to Holyrood until two years later when, for political
reasons, he retired to Austria. Although not of the British Royal
line, the comings and goings of the French family, championed,
of course, by the novelist and lawyer, Sir Walter Scott, caused a

certain amount of curious diversion against an escalating background of European war. But a new era of Anglo-Scottish relations was to be ushered in by the visit of King George IV to Edinburgh in 1822. Stage managed by Sir Walter Scott, this event was uniquely significant at the time since George IV was the first reigning British monarch to set foot in Scotland since Charles I. By now the memory of Culloden was far away, and Scott used his widespread influence to reconcile this plump king with his northern realm. It was Scott who unearthed the Honours of Scotland, which had been taken to Edinburgh Castle after their recovery from Kinneff. For one hundred and eighty-nine years the Scottish Regalia had lain locked up in a chest and forgotten.

A second diplomatic move had been the legalisation of tartan and Highland dress, banned since Culloden to all but a few Highland Regiments who had supported the government. This gave rise to the extravagant Levee which was held at Holyrood for the king, and at which the king, himself, appeared in a voluminous kilt worn over pink tights. The king stayed with the Duke of Buccleuch at Dalkeith Palace and the Scots welcomed him with open arms.

Despite the absence of Royal patronage, the eighteenth century and dawning of the nineteenth century had witnessed a great explosion of art and enlightenment in Scotland. Outstanding painters such as Allan Ramsay and Henry Raeburn came to dominate the art world in the United Kingdom, the former appointed painter-in-ordinary to George III, whom he had painted first as Prince of Wales, and later with Queen Charlotte. Then there were writers, thinkers and architects — George Hume, Adam Smith, Sir William Chambers and the Adam family. It had been a time when great numbers of Highland Scots had left the shores of their homeland in search of wealth and a future in the New World. Under sometimes appalling circumstances they had sailed to the Carolinas, to Nova Scotia, New Zealand and the Far East to lay the foundations for Great Britain's Colonial heritage. When George IV, ignoring the plans of his Irish favourite, the Marchioness Conyngham, chose to visit Edinburgh, he must have been aware that he was inspecting one of the most cultured and civilised cities in Europe, and the Capital of a nation whose influence, through its sons and daughters, was being carried around the World.

*Sir Walter Scott — Scotland's great writer, who masterminded the Royal Visit of 1822.*

*King George IV — the first Hanovarian king to set foot on Scottish soil.*

In its way, therefore, King George's visit was a magnificent publicity stunt for Scotland, and essentially responsible for the subsequent surge of enthusiasm experienced for all things pertaining to the Scots. The King's visit should have been painted by that great artist Sir Henry Raeburn, appointed King's limner and painter in Scotland, but he died the following year and Sir David Wilkie's pictures record the event instead.

It was for the visit that the Royal Company of Archers, formed in 1676, was given its status as Royal Bodyguard for Scotland. The Company of Archers, founded as firearms started to appear, and archery, as a war weapon, began to disappear, emerge at State occasions to this day, and consist of "an influential body of noblemen and country gentlemen, for the purpose

*Hugh Munro's painting of the arrival of King George IV off Portobello, near Edinburgh, in 1822. A great day for Scotland.*

of encouraging the noble and useful recreation of archery". When Queen Elizabeth II visited Scotland after her Coronation in 1952, the Archers presented her with a diamond brooch with three arrows on it. Although in this day and age they could be considered anachronistic and slightly comic, with their green uniforms, this largely elderly body adds great colour to the various pageants associated with the Royal Family in Scotland. Another fascinating development about this period, and very much promoted by the King's visit, was the sudden re-appearance of tartan cloth as a "fashion" Fabric, and herewith lies a tale pertaining to Jacobite history which has never been entirely disproved, but could at the same time have been a monumental

*A print commemorating King George IV's visit to Edinburgh Castle in 1822.*

hoax. And the perpetrators of this possible hoax were the most unlikely couple one could have imagined.

One will recall that when Prince Charles Edward and his wife, Louise of Stolberg, left Rome and took a villa between Pisa and Parma, it was widely rumoured in Jacobite circles that Louise had given birth to a child. The claim is that fearing a possible kidnap attempt from the British government, the child was adopted by Admiral John Carter Allen, and was brought up as his son, Thomas. In the first half of the nineteenth century, there appeared in Scotland an exotic couple, first known as the Stuart Hay brothers, but also known as John Sobieski Stuart and Charles Edward Stuart. These two, with their shoulder length hair, ringletted and bearing a remarkable resemblance to the Stuarts of old, as sons of Thomas Allen, who later changed his name to the Scottish Allan, claimed to be grand-sons of Bonnie Prince Charlie. It is indicative of the emotive fascination inspired by Jacobite followers, that a large body of influential people at that time were prepared to accept the brothers' story without question. John and Charles were welcomed and entertained in the highest social circles of London and Edinburgh, although such as Sir Walter Scott viewed them with cautious cynicism. When the couple were settled in Morayshire, he wrote to his close friend and their neighbour, Sir Thomas Dick Lauder making his views quite plain.

*Now a word in your own private ear, my dear Sir Thomas. I have understood that Messrs Hay Allen are young men of talent, great accomplishments, enthusiasm for Scottish manners, and an exaggerating imagination, which possibly deceives even themselves. I myself saw one of these gentlemen wear the Badge of High Constable of Scotland, which he could have no more right to wear than the Crown. Davidoff used also to amuse us with stories of knighthoods and orders which he saw them wear at Sir William Cumming Gordon's. Now this is all very well, and I conceive people may fall into such dreaming habits easily enough and be very agreeable and talented men in other respects, and may be very amusing companions in the country, but their authority on antiquities must necessarily be a little apocryphal when the faith of MSS rests upon their testimony.*

The manuscript to which Sir Walter referred was one concerning the weave and origin of several tartans which the Sobieski Stuarts authoratively identified with various Highland and Border clans. That is another story, but the brothers claimed that their information came through their father from the Scots College of Douay in France. Their book, *Vestiarium Scoticum*, published in 1845, fact or fiction, forms the basis for many of the Clan tartan designs worn today.

On the death of John, Charles Edward began to call himself Count of Albany, and until his death claimed that he was the rightful King of Great Britain. But there was no shortage of other claimants. One such, and credibly so, was the Chevalier de Roehanstart, the illegitimate son of the Prince de Rohan, and Bonnie Prince Charlie's daughter by Clementina Walkinshaw.

Before his death, Charles had legitimised his daughter with the King of France's ratification, creating her Duchess of Albany. The Chevalier had gone to Scotland in 1816 and made no secret of his origins. To make ends meet, he had taught French, but when his grandmother died and left her estate to the late Cardinal King, he petitioned the Prince Regent, who expressed great fascination, but declined politely to be of assistance. Roehanstart led a colourful life, being a mercenary in the Austrian Army, even becoming a general, but he died in Perthshire the result of a carriage accident in 1854 and is buried in the churchyard of Dunkeld Cathedral, the last credible descendant of the Stuart dynasty.

Obviously King George IV was impressed with what he saw in Scotland, and despite the threat to his family, or possibly influenced by his own loathing of his father, he felt sympathetic towards the Jacobites. He gave Pope Pius VII a contribution towards the cost of Canova's monument to James III and his sons in St Peter's in Rome. In 1824, workmen rebuilding the parish church of St Germain discovered three leaden boxes containing remains of King James II, Queen Mary Beatrice and their daughter, Princess Louise Marie. He arranged that their remains be re-interred at a Ceremony before the Catholic Bishop of Edinburgh, and he erected marble tablets to their memory. In later years, his successor, Queen Victoria would claim to be a Jacobite, and it is amusing to learn that on an occasion when her grandson King George V was staying with the Duke of Atholl at Blair Castle, the two men discussed the Forty-Five. "Your ancestor was wrong," announced the king referring to Lord George Murray, who had advised Prince Charles to retreat from Derby. "Had Charles Edward gone on from Derby, I should not have been King of England today."

*In 1953, on her first visit to Scotland as monarch, the crowds of Edinburgh reacted with an enthusiasm for Her Majesty the Queen much the same as they did for her ancestor, King George IV.*

156

# Victoria and the birth of Balmorality

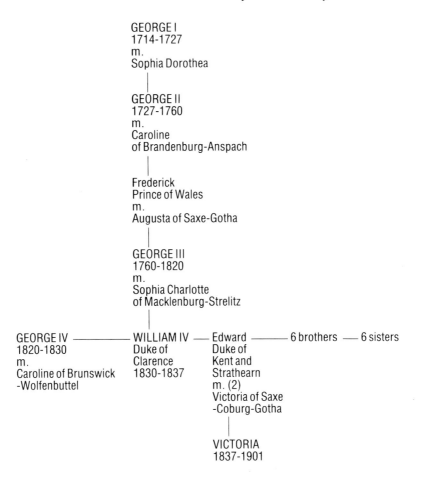

GEORGE I
1714-1727
m.
Sophia Dorothea

GEORGE II
1727-1760
m.
Caroline
of Brandenburg-Anspach

Frederick
Prince of Wales
m.
Augusta of Saxe-Gotha

GEORGE III
1760-1820
m.
Sophia Charlotte
of Macklenburg-Strelitz

GEORGE IV ———————— WILLIAM IV ——— Edward ——————— 6 brothers —— 6 sisters
1820-1830                         Duke of            Duke of
m.                                Clarence           Kent and
Caroline of Brunswick             1830-1837          Strathearn
-Wolfenbuttel                                        m. (2)
                                                     Victoria of Saxe
                                                     -Coburg-Gotha

                                                     VICTORIA
                                                     1837-1901

# 12

## Victoria and the birth of Balmorality

"I FEEL a sort of reverence in going over these scenes in this most beautiful country, which I am proud to call my own, where there was such devoted loyalty to the family of my ancestors — for Stuart blood is in my veins, and I am *now* their representative, and the people are as devoted and loyal to me as they were to that unhappy race." Thus spoke the young Queen Victoria on a visit to her beloved Highlands.

Although certainly a ladies' man, King George IV made no secret of the fact that his wife, Caroline of Brunswick-Wolfenbuttel was a total anathema of him. He seems to have had a sad, although excessive, life — his celebrated confrontations with his father as the old King grew progressively mad, his unhappy marriage, and a series of scandalous and unfulfilling romantic attachments with ambitious society ladies. His true love, Mrs Fitzherbert, besides being a Catholic, could never become his legal wife. And then his only child, Charlotte, married to King Leopold of the Belgians, died in childbirth in 1817.

All this was in marked contrast to his father's prolific marriage to Sophia of Macklenburg-Strelitz. George IV was one of nine brothers and six sisters, and when he died in 1830, next in line to the throne was his sailor brother, the Duke of Clarence who became King William IV. When he died in 1837, after an uneventful reign, the throne passed to their eighteen year old niece, Victoria, daughter of their brother, the Duke of Kent and Strathearn.

Queen Victoria visited Scotland on 31st August 1842, when her Royal Yacht, a converted man-of-war, the *Royal George*, sailed up the East Coast. With her husband, Prince Albert of Saxe-Coburg-Gotha, the Queen had decided upon a Royal Progress that would take her from Edinburgh to Perth and then to the Highlands where they would be guests of the Marquis of Breadalbane at Taymouth Castle.

On 1st September, the Queen stepped ashore at Granton where she was welcomed by the Duke of Buccleuch, who was Captain-General of the Royal Company of Archers. It had been intended that the Royal Party should stay at Holyrood, but it had been some years since the Palace had been occupied and it was generally considered to be far from suitable. Instead, the Duke of Buccleuch played host at his Palace of Dalkeith.

The visit proved an enormous success, both personally enjoyable for the Queen, but also in terms of public relations since lingering Jacobite sympathies were quickly overcome by a glimpse of the vivacious young monarch on her travels. Prince Albert considered Dalkeith "very German-looking" and all the time drew comparisons with his native land. His pleasurable reactions certainly influenced the Queen, but there is little doubt that she herself was falling in love with her northern realm.

At Dunkeld, she was met by the Atholl Highlanders armed with their Lochaber axes. She witnessed a display of Scottish dancing and tasted whisky. At Taymouth Castle, after a great welcome, there was a firework display and in the darkness "Welcome Victoria-Albert" was spelt out by hundreds of oil lamps and bonfires blazed from the surrounding hills.

In the week that followed Prince Albert went deer-stalking and from his report on the subject obviously enjoyed himself enormously. But all too soon the visit was over and the Royal couple returned to London by a steamer, the *Trident*, so new and efficient, it inspired the Queen to order her own, which she named *Victoria and Albert*. Prince Albert was to write of the entire experience in glowing terms:

> *The country is full of beauty, of a severe and grand character; perfect for the sport of all kings, and the air remarkably pure and light; in comparison with what we have here. The people are more natural, and are marked by that honesty and sympathy which always distinguish the inhabitants of mountainous countries.*

Before steaming South, the Queen had employed her own piper, MacKay, and had promised that she would introduce tartan to the fashionable world. In 1844, she returned, this time to spend two weeks at Lord Glenlyon's invitation at Blair Castle.

The *Victoria and Albert* sailed to Dundee, a difficult voyage as the weather was bad. But at Blair, the welcome was again tumultuous. Victoria decided to learn the Gaelic between making pony excursions into the mountains; there were field sports and Highland dances and everybody seemed to have an outstandingly good time. It was then that the Royal Couple decided that Scottish visits should become regular.

In 1847, they leased Ardverikie from the Marquis of Abercorn. This shooting lodge stood on the banks of Loch Laggan, a particularly romantic and remote location. They visited the Clyde this time, landing later at Fort William. On their way they called in on the Duke of Argyll at Inveraray Castle for luncheon, a sudden decision made possible by the prompt action of the Duke's mother-in-law, the Duchess of Sutherland who sent her staff down from Dunrobin Castle to help.

"Alas!" wrote Victoria on her arrival at Ardverikie, "the country is fine, but the weather is most dreadful." The bad weather persisted, but there were Highland gatherings, the young Prince of Wales was dressed up in the Stewart tartan, and Albert also found time to visit Fort Augustus and Inverness, before embarking upon a particularly wet and miserable return journey. And it was this disappointing third visit to Scotland which indicated to them that the climate could not always be guaranteed to be splendid.

Indeed, they might easily have abandoned all plans for future visits had not the son of the Queen's doctor, who had been recovering from an illness on Upper Deeside, reported to his father, who had been watching the grey skies at Ardverikie, that on Upper Deeside there were blue skies and warm sunshine. The Queen was informed and reported to her husband, who in his methodical way asked for a weather report on the area. The report confirmed that on the eastern side of the Cairngorms, there tended to be comparatively little rainfall in the summer months. The Royal Couple's interest was re-awakened, and then it was a stroke of fate which made their dreams possible.

That October, while taking breakfast, Sir Robert Gordon, brother of Lord Aberdeen, a bachelor with a large estate, choked on a fish-bone and died. Some years before, he had acquired the lease of Balmoral Castle from the Earl of Fife's Trustees, and Lord Aberdeen, to whom the estate now passed, suggested that Her Majesty might be interested in taking up the remaining 27 years of the lease. To encourage her, the landscape painter James Giles was commissioned to present three watercolours of the Castle, and the Queen and Prince Albert were delighted.

*Balmoral Castle, Aberdeenshire, purchased by Prince Albert in 1852.*

Balmoral had been a fifteenth century castle, undoubtedly built for defensive purposes. It had come into the hands of the Farquharson of Inverey, a branch of Invercauld, in the 17th century, but after their involvement with the rising of 1715, the Crown had seized the Estate and lordship was granted to the Earl of Fife, who had made substantial alterations, before purchasing the freehold towards the end of the 18th Century for £7020. Between 1834 and 1839, Sir John Gordon virtually demolished the original building and rebuilt Balmoral from plans prepared by John Smith of Aberdeen.

In 1848, Queen Victoria instructed her solicitors to acquire the lease of Balmoral Castle on her husband's behalf. In September, after the now customary arduous journey, but warm welcome, the Royal Couple set eyes on their new home. A Guard of Honour formed by the 93rd Regiment awaited them. That afternoon they walked to the top of the nearest hill overlooking the policies.

"The view from here," wrote the Queen in her journal, "looking down upon the house, is charming. To the left you look towards the beautiful hills surrounding Loch-na-gar, and to the right, towards Ballater, to the glen (or valley) along which the Dee winds, with beautiful wooded hills, which reminded us very much of the Thuringerwald."

The estate at that time consisted of 10,000 acres, to which, in 1849, were added the further 14,000 of the neighbouring Abergeldie Estate. Abergeldie Castle was acquired for the Queen's mother, the Duchess of Kent, and was later used by the Prince of Wales. The estate was brought up to 30,000 acres with the later purchase of Birkhall, consisting of 6000 acres.

On the very first Sunday, the Royal Family set the precedent of attending morning service at Crathie Church, replaced in 1894 by the present church. It was the first step in an informal participation in local activities which has been continued by the Royal Family to the present day. And on another occasion, during their early visits to Balmoral, she attended a Gathering of the Clans held at Braemar.

This annual occasion, claims its origins from the reign of King Malcolm Canmore. It would seem that Malcolm called the Clans to the Braes of Mar for trials of strength, so that he could choose his "hardiest soldiers and his fleetest messengers". By the Nineteenth Century these trials of strength had developed into the more formal contests such as throwing the hammer, tossing the caber and hill racing. On this occasion, at Invercauld House, home of Farquharson of Invercauld, an enormous marquee had been erected, and from here she watched the various events. In the evening there was a Highland Ball.

And in the years that followed a pattern was established. It inevitably caused problems that the Queen of Great Britain should retreat away from her Capital and from her government, and there were the expected communication problems, but one suspects she found a certain pleasure in this. Romantic at heart, she identified herself with the land of her ancestors, and established a new link with the people of that country who had been so sorely neglected by her immediate forebears. She created her second son Duke of Edinburgh in 1866, the first Royal Dukedom with a Scottish title. Her fourth son, Leopold, born 1853, had as his second name 'Duncan' as a "compliment to dear Scotland", and in later years she created him Duke of Albany and saw to it that his first son was named Charles Edward.

But these private visits to Scotland also encompassed official duties and goodwill trips. In 1849, they landed in Glasgow and there was a procession through the streets; in 1850, they opened a viaduct at Berwick and in Edinburgh, where they stayed for two days, they laid the foundation stone for the Royal Scottish

*Queen Victoria and family explore the highlands of Scotland on Shetland ponies.*

Academy, which now stands so splendid at the east end of Princes Street.

Holyrood, by this stage, being restored, was fit for a Queen. "We saw the rooms where Queen Mary lived," noted the Queen in her journal. "Her bed, her dressing room into which the murderers entered who killed Rizzio, and the spot where he fell, where, as the old housekeeper said to me, "if the lady would stand on that side" I would see the boards were discoloured by blood." Despite such evident curiosity, Victoria was not to make great use of Holyrood; it was Balmoral that she considered her Scottish home. And there were many visitors to Balmoral, including the painter Sir Edwin Landseer, who had painted many portraits of members of the Royal Family. He gave sketching lessons to the Queen, and it was here that he conceived 'The Stag at Bay' which epitomises the whole romantic Victorian obsession with the Highlands, the fashionable ideal for every sporting member of Victoria's upper and, indeed, upper-middle class subjects. It became now an essential symbol of prestige to spend Autumn days shooting or stalking in Scotland. But in 1851, Prince Albert still did not own Balmoral, and to enable him to buy the estate, it was necessary, because of the terms of the Earl of Fife's lease, to pass a Private Bill through Parliament.

*An unusual view of Balmoral Castle, showing the Ballroom.*

This Balmoral Estate Act, having been passed on 17th June 1852, enabled Prince Albert to purchase the estate from the Fife Trustees for the sum of £31,500. This coincided with a rather well-timed legacy from an eccentric admirer of the Queen, who left a sum in the region of a quarter of a million pounds for her 'sole use and benefit'. The Queen appeared surprised at the legacy from John Camden Nield, but having had it investigated, accepted and ordered a stained glass window to be added to that gentleman's local church.

Work began in earnest on new building work to plans put forward by William, son of John Smith. To mark their taking possession, a Cairn was built on Craig Gowan, and by the end of 1853, a new castle began to rise behind the old, one hundred yards north, and on a spot which commanded finer views. And once completed, the Queen was able to indulge herself in the most outrageous flights of Celtic design fantasy. Tartan was employed wherever possible, on carpets and on walls, in the servant's quarters, on linoleum. Upholstery bore a thistle motif, also used on bed canopies and curtain pelmets. Lord Clarendon was to note, "the curtains, the furniture, the carpets . . . are all of different plaids, and the thistles are in such abundance that they would rejoice the heart of a donkey." Meanwhile, Prince

Albert, who himself designed a 'Balmoral tartan', set about land-scaping the grounds, and relocating roadways so as to ensure their privacy.

But despite that, Balmoral was frequently used for informal state purposes. Often, serious matters of government took on a clearer aspect in the fresh air and glorious surroundings of Deeside, and Ministers and foreign dignitaries were encouraged to visit. Florence Nightingale was among them, and it was through a meeting here with Lord Panmure, the Secretary of State for War, engineered by the Queen, that a Royal Commission was set up on military hospitals. Victoria and Albert were a devoted couple, and at Balmoral they found the peace and relaxation so elusive in their public lives. Although conscious of a certain amount of displeasure incurred by their being absent from the centre of government each year, in the days when communications were virtually non-existent at the best of times, Balmoral became a necessary annual tonic. Then, not long returned to Windsor after such a retreat, in 1861, the Prince contracted typhoid from the Windsor drains, and on the night of Saturday 14th December, he died. For the Queen, it was as if her world had collapsed all about her.

To begin with many, including herself, thought she would go mad. Widowhood induced her to retreat from public life, desperately searching to recover her spirit through solitude, and it was to Balmoral that she turned for that solitude. To begin with, she was consumed with a need to be surrounded by familiar things such as she had shared with Albert, but by most standards, her mourning was of an enormously self-indulgent and rather over-dramatic nature. However, rulers are creatures apart, and the void left by a soul-mate's departure in such circumstances is something that cannot be filled easily.

In the eyes of Victoria, Balmoral was to become a shrine to her late husband. His forest was to remain perfectly quiet; no heads shot by the Prince were to be removed from the Castle walls, and none added, unless exceptional. "No one knows what her bitter anguish and suffering are — or how that poor heart is pierced and bleeding," she wrote to Lord Palmerston. Balmoral was to remain exactly as it had been when the Prince was alive. In 1863, a memorial pyramid was erected, a massive cairn standing 35 feet high onto which, six years later, was placed a majestic

*Photograph of Queen Victoria by Adam Dickson — she never recovered from the death of her husband, Prince Albert.*

*A recently discovered portrait of John Brown by Carl Sohn jnr, now on display at the Museum of Scottish Tartans in Comrie, Perthshire.*

statue. The inscription reads that it had been erected by the Prince's "Broken hearted widow,"

> *He being made perfect in a short time fulfilled a long time;*
> *For his soul pleased the Lord,*
> *Therefore hastened He to take him*
> *Away from among the wicked.*     (Wisdom of Solomon.)

But as distance was put between the present and that unhappy bereavement, the Queen's spirits began to rally. It was becoming public knowledge that she had found a soul-mate of sorts to fill her lonely days.

John Brown was not, as has often been suggested, the son of a crofter. His father was a schoolteacher, himself the son of a small landowner on Deeside. John, born in 1826, was one of eleven children, and had been employed at Balmoral by Sir Robert Gordon, thus being a member of the staff taken over by

Prince Albert. To begin with his duties had included being a stable-boy, then gillie. In later years he was to lead the Royal expeditions into the hills, and at the age of 37, Victoria appointed him her 'Personal Servant'. "It is a real comfort to me, she announced, "for he is so devoted to me — so simple, so intelligent, so unlike an ordinary servant, and so cheerful and attentive."

Such was the rise of this inscrutable Highlander that in 1879, the Queen re-titled him "Personal Attendant and Page", endowing him with a servant of his own and a specially built house, Baile-na-Coile. Naturally, such favouritism gave rise to gossip, and it is known that the Prince of Wales loathed his mother's servant, and in later years had Brown's statue removed to a less public part of the estate. Nobody will ever know what the relationship between this monarch and servant encompassed. Brown was certainly most informal when speaking with the Queen, but there is no evidence that they were intimate in other ways. Brown with his love of country pursuits certainly reminded the Queen of Prince Albert; he was reliable and handsome in a rough, manly way. If he had any identifiable faults, he enjoyed his whisky, but then the Queen, herself, was not impartial to a dram or two.

Inevitably, John Brown's sudden death in 1883, was as devastating an experience as the death of her late husband. He was mourned as "a trustworthy, discreet, and straightforward man possessed of strong sense". The Queen wrote that she was "utterly crushed".

John Brown was buried at Crathie, and Sir Joseph Boehm commissioned to produce a life-size sculpture. The inscription on this reads: "Friend more than Servant, Loyal, Truthful, Brave, Self less than Duty, even to the Grave". The Queen embodied the outrageous sentimentality so popular during her reign, and to Balmoral's embarrassed factor Dr Profeit, she presented a tie pin which incorporated a miniature of Brown, set in diamonds.

As the Royal Family grew up, Balmoral became an annual gathering ground for them and the many relatives, representatives of Europe's Crowned Heads, by marriage. Empress Eugenie of France, descended from the Royal Stuart line through her mother's descent from the Duke of Berwick and Alva, principal Grandee of Spain, came often to Scotland. She loved the "transparent, washed sky, its green moors, its lakes scattered everywhere like sprinkled drops of the purest water". She visited Abbotsford, Edinburgh and the Trossachs, and stayed with the

# DÉJEÛNER

### ON THE OCCASION OF THE OPENING OF

## The International Exhibition, Edinburgh.

### By their Royal Highnesses The Duke & Duchess of Edinburgh.

## MENU

1st MAY       1890.

**CHAIRMAN—**
Sir THOMAS CLARK, *Bart.*,
*Chairman of the Executive Council.*

**CROUPIERS—**

Councillor KINLOCH ANDERSON, J.P.
Professor ARMSTRONG, C.E.
Councillor BARCLAY, J.P.
A. R. BENNETT, Esq., F.R.S.E.
B. HALL BLYTH, Esq., C.E.
MITCHELL THOMSON, Esq.

*Vice-Chairmen of the Executive Council.*

---

POUCHEAU RHUM
AMONTILLADO

HOCKS—
  Marcobrunner, 1874
  Hockheimer, 1874

CHAMPAGNES—
  Ruinart, Pere &
    Fils, 1880
  Irroy, 1884
  de Lossy, 1884

VINO DE PASTO

FINE OLD PORT—
  Croft's Particular

CLARET—
  Chateau Leoville
  Barton, 1874

WYNAND FOCKINCK's
LIQUEURS

### POTAGE.
CONSOMME A LA DUCHESS.

### POISSONS.
SAUMON A L'ECOSSAISE.
MAYONNAISE DE HOMARD.
FILETS DE SOLES A L'ORLY.

### ENTREES.
CHAUDFROIDS DE PRINTADES A LA PRINCESSE
POULETS DECOUPS ET LANGUES.
MOUSSE DE FOIE A LA MODERNE.
JAMBON DE BAYONNE HISTORIE.
GALANTINES DE DINDE AUX TRUFFES.
PATE DE GIBIER A L'ECOSSAISE.
COTELETTES D'AGNEAU AUX CONCOMBRES.
FILET DE BŒUF A LA GELEE.
LANGUE ECARLATE.
QUARTIERS D'AGNEAU, SCE. MENTHE.
PIECE DE BŒUF A LA CHASSEUR.

### ROTIS.
ASPERGES GLACEES A LA IMPERATRICE.
ŒUFS DE PLUVIERS EN PYRAMIDE
SALADE FRANCAISE.

### ENTREMETS.
GATEAU NAPOLITAIN.
CHARLOTTE RUSSE, AUX PISTACHES.
CREME BAVAROISE A L'ALBERT.
CROQUEMBOUCHE D'ORANGES.
GATEAU ST HONORE.
GELEES AUX CHAMPAGNE.
PATISSERIE PARISIENNE.

POUDING GLACE, A LA MANCHESTER.

### DESSERT.
CORBEILLE DE FRUITS FRAIS.

---

## TOASTS

THE QUEEN.
THE PRINCE AND PRINCESS OF WALES.
THE DUKE AND DUCHESS OF EDINBURGH, AND OTHER MEMBERS OF THE
ROYAL FAMILY.

**A. MACKENZIE ROSS, Purveyor.**

W. Adamson, Litho.

Duchess of Hamilton at Hamilton Palace in Lanarkshire. She enjoyed a close personal friendship with Victoria, staying also at Balmoral, and when the Second Empire fell in 1871, the Queen offered her Abergeldie Castle on Deeside as a Highland home.

Among the Queen's relatives to visit Balmoral was her favourite grandson, the future Kaiser Wilhelm of Germany, and as a sign of her favour, he was permitted to wear the Stewart tartan. And then there was the Tsar of Russia in 1896. This was, in effect, a State Visit, and the attendant Royalty presented an impressive indication of the British Royal Family's role in Europe. They included Prince Charles of Denmark, later King Haakon of Norway; the Princess of Wales, a daughter of the King of Denmark; Princess Maud, later Queen of Denmark, and Princess Margaret of Connaught, later Crown Princess of Sweden. The Russian Royal Family was doubly connected. The Queen's son, the Duke of Edinburgh had married the former Tsar's daughter, Marie. His heir, Tsar Nicholas II, had married his cousin, Princess Alix, youngest daughter of Princess Alice, Grand Duchess of Hesse, Victoria's second daughter. This unhappy couple would later perish in the storm of the Bolshevik Revolution.

Thus it was that Victoria's latter years at Balmoral were spent in the company of her large family. She died at Osborne on 22nd January 1901, having passed her eighty-first birthday at Balmoral the year before. Then she had appeared frail, but had made her customary trip around the Estate cottages, although this time she had not left her carriage. The Highlanders knew then that she would not return.

*A souvenir menu commemorating the visit of Queen Victoria's second son and his wife to the International Exhibition held in Edinburgh in 1890.*

# *The Twentieth Century*

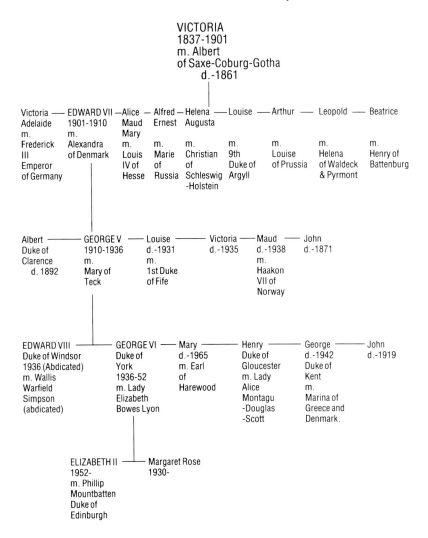

VICTORIA
1837-1901
m. Albert
of Saxe-Coburg-Gotha
d.-1861

| Victoria | EDWARD VII | Alice | Alfred | Helena | Louise | Arthur | Leopold | Beatrice |
|---|---|---|---|---|---|---|---|---|
| Adelaide | 1901-1910 | Maud | Ernest | Augusta | | | | |
| m. | m. | Mary | | | | | | |
| Frederick | Alexandra | m. | m. | m. | m. | m. | m. | m. |
| III | of Denmark | Louis | Marie | Christian | 9th | Louise | Helena | Henry of |
| Emperor | | IV of | of | of | Duke of | of Prussia | of Waldeck | Battenburg |
| of Germany | | Hesse | Russia | Schleswig | Argyll | | & Pyrmont | |
| | | | | -Holstein | | | | |

| Albert | GEORGE V | Louise | Victoria | Maud | John |
|---|---|---|---|---|---|
| Duke of | 1910-1936 | d.-1931 | d.-1935 | d.-1938 | d.-1871 |
| Clarence | m. | m. | | m. | |
| d. 1892 | Mary of | 1st Duke | | Haakon | |
| | Teck | of Fife | | VII of | |
| | | | | Norway | |

| EDWARD VIII | GEORGE VI | Mary | Henry | George | John |
|---|---|---|---|---|---|
| Duke of Windsor | Duke of | d.-1965 | Duke of | d.-1942 | d.-1919 |
| 1936 (Abdicated) | York | m. Earl | Gloucester | Duke of | |
| m. Wallis | 1936-52 | of | m. Lady | Kent | |
| Warfield | m. Lady | Harewood | Alice | m. | |
| Simpson | Elizabeth | | Montagu | Marina of | |
| (abdicated) | Bowes Lyon | | -Douglas | Greece and | |
| | | | -Scott | Denmark. | |

| ELIZABETH II | Margaret Rose |
|---|---|
| 1952- | 1930- |
| m. Phillip | |
| Mountbatten | |
| Duke of | |
| Edinburgh | |

# 13

## The Twentieth Century

THE special attachment of Queen Victoria and Prince Albert to Scotland imprinted itself strongly on the minds of their family. Princess Louise, the one child not married off to a scion of European Royalty, married John Douglas Sutherland Campbell, 9th Duke of Argyll in 1871, and her home, therefore, became the fairytale Inveraray Castle on the shores of Loch Fyne. As Marquess of Lorne, the Duke had served as a Member of Parliament, and seven years after their marriage, he was appointed Governor General of Canada. There were, however, no children from this marriage, and when the Duke died, the title passed to a relative.

The Prince of Wales had been born at Buckingham Palace in 1841, and it had been a long wait before he inherited his throne. Educated by a number of learned men at home, he then studied Chemistry at Edinburgh University under Professor (later Lord) Playfair. In 1860, he was permitted to visit the United States of America and Canada, rather curiously using the title of Lord Renfrew. But it was a far from easy existence for a Prince of considerable intelligence and ability. For many years he had to content himself with being constantly in his mother's shadow, while the Queen, despite her retreat from public life, steadfastly refused to delegate the administrative duties of her position. Instead, the Prince was encouraged to travel. Having completed a course at Cambridge, a year after his father's death, he went on a tour of the Holy Land under the guidance of Arthur Penrhyn Stanley, who later became Dean of Westminster. In 1863, he took his place in the House of Lords as Duke of Cornwall, but it was a constant requirement that he should avoid commitment.

And it is true to say that Balmoral had a certain place in his affections, although he described it as "the place of a thousand drafts". The Prince, like his father, was an enthusiastic sportsman, and early on in his life the estate of Sandringham had been purchased for him out of the savings of his minority. Away from London, therefore, this became his first choice as home, although he continued the tradition of visiting Deeside each Autumn.

In 1863, Edward married Princess Alexandra, the lovely daughter of King Christian IX of Denmark. Parliament granted him an income of £40,000 per annum, exclusive to his Cornwall revenues, and he relinquished his right of succession to the duchy of Saxe-Coburg-Gotha. Naturally the Nation took a great interest in this handsome couple, particularly with the Queen so much out of sight. But the Prince's role continued to remain ceremonial.

He visited Egypt with the Duke of Sutherland and he opened the International Exhibition in Ireland in 1871. In 1875, the Royal couple toured India and in 1890 he officially opened the Forth Rail Bridge, one of the most remarkable engineering triumphs of its day.

But it is hardly surprising that this continual role of "showing the flag", representing his mother as "heir-apparent" for over forty years caused him considerable frustration. His private life became filled with flirtations with beautiful women, gambling and extravagant living. There were echoes of that former Prince of Wales who became King George IV, and Edward's friends and activities often encountered his mother's pronounced disapproval. Yet his marriage remained intact and he gained a certain "racy" affection from the people. He was a great supporter of the theatre and always an enthusiastic sportsman on several fronts. His horses twice won the Derby, and later when he had his third victory with his horse Minorus, it was the first time a reigning sovereign had won such an event. At the same time, he was a keen yachtsman, and his yacht *Britannia* took part in many important fixtures.

With such an active leisure life and no great official responsibilities, it was inevitable that the Prince should be prey to gossip. In 1890, he became involved in the Tranby Croft Case in which a Morayshire landowner, Sir William Gordon Cumming, brought an unsuccessful libel action for having been accused of cheating at the game of baccarat. The Prince's appearance in the witness box on behalf of the defendants caused a scandal in respectable Victorian Britain and it was widely concluded that Sir

William was innocent and that the Prince's true role in the business was far from honest.

One figure emerges from this period with great stature and this was the Princess of Wales, later Queen Alexandra. A beautiful, dignified figure, she remained devoted to her husband and bore him six children, although they were soon to be faced with a sad domestic tragedy.

In 1892, Prince Albert, Duke of Clarence, the eldest son and heir-presumptive, died after a brief illness. The Prince had recently become engaged to Princess Victoria Mary of Teck, and the alliance was widely praised. The young Princess Mary was popular with the Royal Family, and such is the way of things that the following year she married the second son, Prince George, Duke of York. Meanwhile, the policy of Royal alliances bringing about stability with allies continued, and in 1896, Princess Maud, Edward and Alexandra's third daughter, married Prince Charles of Denmark and was later to become Queen of Norway. Surprisingly, such a match was not mandatory for the eldest daughter, the Princess Royal, who was able to marry Alexander Duff, 6th Earl and created Duke of Fife, whose home was at Mar Lodge, so near to Balmoral.

King Edward, influenced by his early years, undoubtedly travelled about more than any of his predecessors. In consequence, therefore, he was able to spend little time in any one place. His first official visit to Scotland as King took place in May 1903, when he held court at Holyrood, but then that same year he also visited Lisbon, Gibraltar, Malta, Rome, Paris, Ireland, Marienbad and Vienna. It is not surprising that with his diplomatic initiatives he became known as "Edward the Peacemaker" and by some as "Edward the Pacemaker".

But King Edward's visits to Balmoral lacked the significance of his parent's time, and despite the introduction of the Motor Car which marked the way for so many changes of the early Twentieth Century, Balmoral's role as a Royal home decreased in importance, particularly with the approach of the First World War. The days of Prime Ministers travelling to see the monarch on urgent matters of state no matter where the monarch was located, were over. Postal services, the telegram and telephone were taking over, and Parliament was forging a far more independant role for itself. Although King Edward and his successor, King George V maintained enormous influence over government, Ministers would never again be as subservient as they had been in the time of Victoria.

King Edward died in 1910 following a bronchial attack. His

funeral, attended by the German Emperor, the Kings of Spain, Greece, Denmark, Portugal, Norway, Belgium and Bulgaria, the Prince Consort of Holland and the Arch-Duke Ferdinand of Austria, all of whom were related in some way, was a remarkable pageant marking almost the end of an era dominated by the British Monarchy and its Empire. Sweeping political change was about to take place in Europe; Kings, Tsars and Emperors would lose their thrones, and after the totality of the 1914-1918 War, nothing would ever be the same again. Already the unrest in Russia was building up towards the revolution which would bring about the fall of the Tsar and the murder of Queen Victoria's grand-daughter. In Germany, Queen Victoria's grand-son, the Kaiser, was seeking to expand his influence and the entire question of the role of kings in government and the existence of a British House of Lords was under attack. King George V, who as a youth had fished the pools of the Dee with a passion, was also an excellent shot and enjoyed stalking. But the early years of his reign were to afford him few opportunities to take refuge at Balmoral, particularly when war broke out.

In the 'Twenties, it became a feature that Prime Ministers would visit Balmoral for a weekend each year, and for the first time Socialist ministers were invited to stay. But the crowds who gathered for a glimpse of the Royal Family either on the estate or at worship at Crathie were becoming a nuisance, detracting from the privacy of the retreat. Despite this, Autumn holidays in Scotland continued and improvements were made, such as the commissioning of the fine gate from local craftsmen. Queen Mary created a rose garden which carried her name.

King George V died at Sandringham in 1936 greatly mourned. He had brought an astute and respected authority to his position in difficult times. Such events as the General Strike of 1926 could have brought about revolution, but it is widely held that the influencing stability of the Head of State helped to balance sanity against civil strife, and this role as a personage above politics, yet symbolising the status and security of the Nation had by then evolved as the most significant duty of the monarchy. Whereas other kings in Europe sought to interfere with the management of their countries against rising political influences, and therefore failed, the British Royal Family survives by giving the Nation a solid, respectable base upon which the most radical reforms can be debated, accepted or rejected by majority opinion. And it is true to say that this approach was largely instigated by King George V, a far sighted and profoundly dedicated man.

The constitutional crisis concerning the succession of King

Edward VIII affected Scotland as much as it did Great Britain as a whole. This Prince of Wales had been born at Windsor in 1894, and was generally popular throughout the country. In 1933, he had visited various mutual service institutions for the unemployed in Scotland, and the same year had visited Rothesay, where, as the Duke of that name, he received a great welcome. Aside from that, his interests and activities were in no way exclusive to Scotland.

What was to prove far more significant was the marriage of his younger brother, the Duke of York, to Lady Elizabeth Bowes Lyon, daughter of the 14th Earl of Strathmore and Kinghorne.

Lady Elizabeth Bowes Lyon was born in England and her childhood was split between St Paul's Walden, in Hertfordshire, and dark, forbidding Glamis Castle with its red sandstone walls, its legends and intrigues, set in the rolling countryside of Angus. This was the first of two Scottish Royal marriages by this generation for Prince Henry, the Duke of Gloucester, in 1935 married Lady Alice Montagu-Douglas-Scott, 3rd daughter of the 7th Duke of Buccleuch, thus re-newing the Royal connection with that family which dates back to the Duke of Monmouth. The marriage in 1923 between the shy second son of King George V and the lively Lady Elizabeth, however, was to prove one of the most happy, and fortunate liaisons. There had been no thought of their becoming King and Queen; no doubt that the Prince of Wales would eventually marry and produce heirs. But in 1937, the new King Edward's announced intention to marry an American divorcee, a prospect at that time bitterly at conflict with all the established values of Church and Establishment, brought protest throughout the land. The ensuing abdication found the withdrawn and sensitive Duke of York taking up his Crown as King George VI, and it was entirely through his efforts and the charm and energy of his consort that once again the British Royal family was restored to credibility and affection in the hearts of the British people. And the new Queen was intensely proud of being Scottish, influencing the placement of the Scottish lion rampant on the back of alternate shillings in her husband's new coinage and insisting that her second child, Princess Margaret Rose should be born at her parent's home in Scotland. It is interesting to note that only one member of the Royal Family has been born at Balmoral, and that was Victoria Eugenie, daughter of Queen Victoria's youngest daughter, Princess Beatrice, who had married Prince Henry of Battenburg. Victoria Eugenie, who married King Alfonso of Spain, as an exile in Lausanne in the 1950s was extremely proud of her Scottish birth.

And so it is with Queen Elizabeth the Queen Mother, although not, of course, having been born in Scotland. When approached by a South African at a reception who informed her "I must tell you, Ma'am, that I detest the English," she replied, without hestitation, "Oh I do so understand. You see I am Scottish".

Such sentiment, coupled with an obvious enthusiasm for country life, has made her much loved in Scotland. The first State Visit of 1937 was a tremendous success, and one of the first actions was to unveil a granite obelisk to launch Scotland's Empire Exhibition scheduled for 1940.

They visited Newhaven's Gala Day, and as had been the case in both Glasgow and Edinburgh, the streets were filled with colourful, cheering crowds. Twenty three thousand children paraded at Murrayfield before a crowd of some 20,000, and 8,000 guests attended the garden party at Holyrood. It was as if a King and Queen had truly returned to the Scottish people; a King and Queen who were to be much loved and, as had Victoria, to prove that they returned that love. And as a symbol of Royal respect for Scotland, and no doubt affection for his wife, the King restored the regular installation of Knights of the Thistle, investing as one of his first, his father-in-law, Lord Strathmore.

The Most Ancient and Most Noble Order of the Thistle is the second in precedence of the British Orders of Chivalry. It is the Scottish equivalent of the Garter and is of even greater antiquity. The Order was formerly assigned to the Chapel Royal at Holyrood and consisted of the Sovereign and twelve knights. The number was increased to 16 in 1821 and, in 1911, the splendid Thistle Chapel at the south-east corner of St Giles Cathedral in Edinburgh was completed and dedicated.

In 1919, as Duke of York, King George had suggested that boys between seventeen and nineteen from industrial firms and from Public Schools, should come together for an annual camp as his guests. In 1939, the chosen site was in the grounds of Abergeldie Castle, and on this occasion, on the very eve of the Second World War, the King himself led expeditions each day, including one to the top of Lochnagar. The boys had tea at Balmoral and the Royal Family joined the boys for supper in their camp. It was obvious that the King loved the informality of such occasions and it was to be the way of things to come in the

*King George VI and Queen Elizabeth at the Braemar Gathering, continuing a family tradition.*

*Balmoral Castle continued to be an informal meeting place for chosen guests, in this case, the Australian Cricket team.*

post war years, and particularly at Balmoral. The stiff formalities of the Court were on their way out; the monarchy was learning to mix with and come closer to its people. In doing so, the image was becoming more identifiable and something which the British people could relate to themselves.

Claude Muncaster, the painter, was a visitor in 1947. The King admired Muncaster's work and had invited him to be their guest and paint views of the landscape around the estate. In *The Wind on the Oak*, Martin Muncaster records his father's impressions.

"When we joined the ladies after dinner," he wrote, "we found Princess Margaret playing the piano and singing in a powerful voice. She was doing a most entertaining turn which closely resembled a Gracie Fields' act. Princess Elizabeth, who adores her sister and thinks all she does marvellous, was rolling on the rug by the piano in paroxysms of laughter. When this turn was completed, the Queen asked me to sing something. I

*A young Princess Elizabeth delights at the sound of the Pipes in the grounds of Balmoral.*

could scarcely refuse a Royal Command so, greatly to my embarrassment, I gave my rendering of Deep River. I sang extremely badly and my bottom notes seemed to have disappeared. I suppose embarrassment and champagne had drowned them. Following this unfortunate anti-climax to an otherwise most enjoyable evening, I was surprised to see a tartan shawl put over the firescreen; to hear that two detectives had been chosen; to find the lights suddenly turned out and the whole house party involved in a game of "Murders". When the last person had been murdered and the murderer discovered in the shape of Sir Alan Lascelles, it was well nigh one o'clock and everybody retired to bed."

King George VI's death in 1952 brought to the throne his eldest daughter Elizabeth. In 1947, she had married the son of Prince and Princess Andrew of Greece, therefore a great-great grandson of Queen Victoria. It proved an ideal match. Prince Philip, given the title of Duke of Edinburgh, had been educated at Gordonstoun School in the north of Scotland, and was able to give the young Queen the needed strength to take on the

*Above: King George VI and family at the Braemar Gathering.*

*Opposite: Queen Elizabeth, Princess Elizabeth, Princess Margaret Rose and corgis being welcomed by the Marquis of Aberdeen at Ballater Station.*

enormity of her inheritance at such a young age. The parallel can only be drawn with Victoria and Albert.

And like Prince Albert, Prince Philip takes a serious and active role in the running of Balmoral estate, which under his control, and with his family's enthusiasm has enjoyed something of a renaissance. In 1955, he introduced Highland cattle; in 1966, a herd of Luing cattle, Shorthorns crossed with Highland. In 1972, a herd of Galloways was purchased, and generally farming technology has been applied to get the best out of what amounts to a relatively small Highland estate.

The Queen Mother has made Birkhall on the Balmoral estate her home, and she, also, is a fishing devotee, having the opportunity to fish some of the best stretches of river in Aberdeenshire. In the far North, in Caithness, she early on had purchased the Castle of Mey, where she delights in the wild, scenic coastline.

The Castle of Mey dates from 1606 and is a former Clan Sinclair stronghold. The Queen Mother says that she fell in love

*The Castle of Mey, purchased by Queen Elizabeth the Queen Mother in 1952.*

with it at first sight and it is certainly now the most northern Royal residence, commanding fine views across the Pentland Firth towards Orkney. Although she is unable to make as much use of it as she would perhaps like, it remains a very private home, and only the gardens are open to the public at certain times of year.

The most recent Scottish marriage in the Royal Family of today was between King George V's grand-daughter, Princess Alexandra of Kent, daughter of George, Duke of Kent, who had married Princess Marina of Greece. In 1963, she married the Hon. Angus James Bruce Ogilvy, second son of the 12th Earl of Airlie. The House of Airlie has its roots entwined for centuries with the history of Scotland, having branched off in the 12th century from the great House of Angus, whose head ranked first among the seven Mormaers from whom the mediaeval kingdom was traditionally built up. In fact, their respective lines both connect back to Jean Stewart, King Robert II's daughter by Elizabeth Mure, who married Sir John Lyon of Glamis, and it is just such an example which helps us to understand how closely interlinked are the genealogies of Scotland's families.

*Birkhall Lodge, the Queen Mother's residence on the Balmoral Estate.*

*Above: Prince Philip, Duke of Edinburgh, son of Prince and Princess Andrew of Greece, adapts well to Scottish life.*

*Opposite: A traditional annual visit to Edinburgh where the Royal Family take up residence at Holyrood Palace.*

# The Future

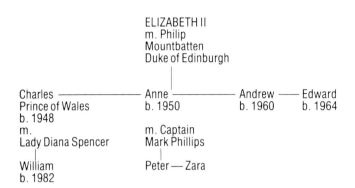

ELIZABETH II
m. Philip
Mountbatten
Duke of Edinburgh

Charles ——————— Anne ——————— Andrew ——— Edward
Prince of Wales          b. 1950              b. 1960       b. 1964
b. 1948
m.                            m. Captain
Lady Diana Spencer    Mark Phillips

William                      Peter —— Zara
b. 1982

# 14

## The Future

IT has to be appreciated that dating from James VI's departure from Scotland in 1603, the British Royal Family's role in the Scottish context has become progressively less political and administrative culminating in the largely symbolic and ceremonial status which it occupies today.

The Silver Jubilee parades which took place through the streets of Edinburgh and Glasgow in 1977 were remarkable in their turnout of cheering, enthusiastic Scots. But one wonders if many realised just what a fascinating pageant they were watching, for before them passed in the various coaches and carriages persons representing great passages of Scotland's history. Each individual in those processions signified some historical office of unique importance, and although today purely ceremonial, their presence returned us to the past, helping us to appreciate just how enduring the traditions of our country have been.

For example, in the first carriage, the Balmoral Landau, two pursuivants of the Court of the Lord Lyon, in their Royal tabards, accompanied the Earl of Lauderdale, Saltire Banner bearer for Scotland. The Earl of Dundee, whose ancestor was granted a charter from Sir William Wallace, Guardian of the Kingdom, appointing him Constable of Dundee and hereditary standard-bearer carried the Royal Banner of Scotland. This Charter was confirmed by Robert Bruce and is the only document in which Bruce mentions Wallace, recognising him as his predecessor in authority. Sir Alexander Scrymgeour to whom these Charters were granted was captured in 1306 and hanged for carrying the Royal Lyon Rampant Banner in battle for King

Robert Bruce. It is appropriate then that his descendant Lord Dundee now carries that same banner for our Queen today.

In the second carriage, the Russian Sociable, travelled the Lord Lyon King of Arms and two heralds, Marchmont and Albany. The Lord Lyon is head of heraldic matters in Scotland, his duties to organise such public ceremonies, to maintain legal control of armorial rights and to record the geneology of the families of Scotland. His office dates back to that of the High Sennachie of the ancient kings of the Gaels, and at Scotland's last coronation, that of King Charles II at Scone, the Lord Lyon, in the traditional manner, recited the king's lineage back to Fergus, first King of Scots in the 6th century.

In the fourth carriage, a Semi-State Landau, sat the Lord High Commissioner to the General Assembly of Scotland. This appointment is made annually by the Crown, and the Commissioner represents the monarch, is styled Your Grace, and takes precedence over all except the monarch, including other members of the Royal Family. Accompanying him was the Purse Bearer, whose purse contains the Royal Commission. The present Lord Chamberlain of the Realm was also in attendance, and, in fact, is a Scot, none other than Lord Maclean of Duart, 27th Chief of Clan Maclean. Two other chiefs accompanied him, although bearing hereditary offices. The Duke of Argyll, chief of Clan Campbell, carried the baton of Hereditary Master of the Royal Household in Scotland; an office held by his family since 1464, but made a hereditary post in 1528 by King James V. In the same carriage was also the Hereditary Lord High Constable of Scotland in the person of the Earl of Erroll, although at the time Master of Erroll representing his mother. The Lord High Constable is primarily responsible for the safety of the Sovereign's person on such occasions and the office was conferred by King Robert Bruce on Sir Gilbert Hay, Lord Erroll after Bannockburn in 1314. To many these personages and their respective relevance might seem anachronistic, and yet they are what makes Scotland so unique. Each and every civilisation needs its structure and traditions, and the presence on such an occasion of representatives of families, who, like our Royal Family have played key roles in the turbulent creation of our Nation gives great continuity, indeed credibility, to the security

*Opposite: Her Majesty inspects her Bodyguard for Scotland, the Royal Company of Archers, founded in 1676.*

and on-going passage of that Nation. The role of Sovereign embodies this credibility; a figurehead above politics, yet recognised the world over as representative of a people. And despite the existence of a united England, Wales, Northern Ireland and Scotland or, for that matter, a British Empire, one should not ignore the fact that the Prince of Wales himself holds the titles of Duke of Rothesay, Earl of Carrick and Lord of the Isles, that most romantic of Highland designations. Sir Iain Moncreiffe of the Ilk, a most distinguished historian and himself, Marchmont Herald, informs us that Prince Charles descends from Mary Queen of Scots no less than twenty-two times over, through various cousin marriages within the ancestry of King George V and Queen Mary, also by many other separate blood lines leading through Prince Philip.

Like their father, the Prince of Wales, Prince Andrew and Prince Edward attended Gordonstoun School founded by Dr Kurt Hahn on the Moray Firth, in 1934. Hahn had been Headmaster at Salem School in Germany, but had taken leave of Nazi Germany with contempt. He had little time for educationalists who believed that children should be allowed to do as they pleased and not compelled to undertake difficult tasks. Equally, he rejected the theory that an individual should be subordinated to the considered good of the whole. At Gordonstoun he devised a system where physical fitness and achievement ran parallel with academic pursuits.

The open air existence obviously has agreed with the Princes who all share an enthusiasm for action. Prince Charles, in particular, loves the fishing, the walking and the freedom available to him at Balmoral. Referring to Queen Victoria and Balmoral, he is quoted as saying: "She hated leaving, much as I hate leaving this marvellous place".

In 1980, he married Lady Diana Spencer, youngest daughter of Earl Spencer. Her lineage is profoundly English, her kinsmen including the Dukes of Richmond, Grafton and Marlborough, but also Abercorn, a title belonging to the Hamilton family. At the same time, her mother, Mrs Frances Shand Kydd, daughter of the 4th Barron Fermoy and Ruth, Lady Fermoy, lives with her second husband on the Island of Seil on the Firth of Lorn. One suspects that the Princess of Wales might not choose to become so active as her husband in the sporting pursuits associated with

*The Princess of Wales' Tam O' Shanter bonnet brings a cheer from the Braemar crowd.*

*Above: The Prince of Wales enjoys a day fishing on the River Dee.*

*Opposite: The Princess of Wales, on the other hand, is not quite so certain.*

Highland life, but it was obvious from the start that she relished the peace and informality of the Balmoral retreat. Indeed, part of their honeymoon was spent on the Estate, affording them a degree of privacy away from the clamouring photographers and reporters of the world press.

The birth of Prince William Arthur Philip Louis ensures the succession of the House of Windsor through the line of the Prince of Wales. And it is certain that the Balmoral tradition will continue with attendance at the Braemar Gathering and Sunday worship at the little church of Crathie.

The Duke of Edinburgh is often found Carriage Driving at

*The Prince and Princess of Wales arrive at the Gordon Highlanders' Regimental Museum for cocktails prior to a Regimental Ball.*

Scone Palace, or at Mellerstain House, the splendid Borders Adam mansion belonging to Lord Binning. The Prince of Wales also visits Scone to play Polo. Princess Margaret, Princess Anne and Princess Alexandra are great favourites in Glasgow and Edinburgh where they regularly attend official functions, and the Ogilvy children often visit their cousins in Angus. Princess Anne and her husband, Captain Mark Phillips, are regular competitors at horse trials in Dumfriesshire and Ayrshire, and Princess Margaret, in particular, likes to attend the Edinburgh Festival and on many such occasions has stayed as guest with the Tennant family at The Glen, Innerleithen.

Each summer, the Queen is resident at Holyrood, where she continues the tradition of the Royal Garden Party and embarks upon an energetic round of official duties; opening factories, visiting hospitals, supporting Charity, possibly attending a Regimental function at which she takes up her role as Colonel-in-Chief. At a recent ceremony, the Earl of Elgin, twice her Lord High Commissioner to the General Assembly, and with whom

*Opposite: The modern role of Royalty — Prince Charles visits an oil rig off the coast of Aberdeen.*

she shares the mutual ancestry of Robert Bruce's forebears, was created Knight of the Thistle.

The Royal Family as it belongs to England, Wales, Northern Ireland and the Commonwealth, is very much Scotland's own Royal Family, an example of stability, indeed, durability against turbulent times. The associated traditions and pageantry are part of the fabric of our Society and, in a changing universe, we should cherish such as part of our birthright and identity as a people. Whatever role the monarch and her descendants come to play in the future, one should always remember that they represent over fifteen hundred years of Scotland's history, carrying forward the duties and dignity of our mutual ancestors, without which, and without whom, the story of our island race would unquestionably have remained uninspired, insignificant and unsung.

*Prince William is carried onto the tarmac of Dyce Airport by a proud father.*

*The Prince and Princess of Wales arrive at Elphinstone Hall, Aberdeen, to attend the eve of departure Ball of the Gordon Highlanders.*

*Her Majesty the Queen pictured during a recent visit to Fochabers, Morayshire.*

# Recommended Reading

*The Story of Scotland.* Janet Glover (Faber & Faber).
*King Hereafter.* Dorothy Dunnett (Michael Joseph).
*A Concise History of Scotland.* Fitzroy Maclean (Thames & Hudson).
*King James IV of Scotland.* R.L. Mackie (Oliver & Boyd).
*The Young Pretender's Mistress.* C. Leo Berry (Charles Skilton).
*Balmoral — Queen Victoria's Highland Home.* Ronald W. Clark (Thames & Hudson).
*Montrose — The King's Champion.* Max Hastings (Victor Gollancz).
*A Highland History.* Earl of Cromartie (Gavin Press).
*James VI of Scotland.* Caroline Bingham (Weidenfeld & Nicolson).
*The Kings and Queens of Scotland.* Caroline Bingham (Weidenfeld & Nicolson).
*The Windsor Tapestry.* Compton Mackenzie (The Book Club).
*Mary, Queen of Scots.* Antonia Fraser (Weidenfeld & Nicolson).
*Charles II — The Man and the Statesman.* Maurice Ashley (Weidenfeld & Nicolson).
*William & Mary.* Henri & Barbara van der Zee (Macmillan).
*The Cardinal King.* Brian Fothergill (Faber & Faber).
*Clan Donald.* Donald J. Macdonald of Castleton (Macdonald).
*The Private Life of the Tudors.* (Selected & Edited). Christopher Falkus (The Folio Society).
*The Scottish World.* Orel Snyder Stokstad (Thames & Hudson).
*Kings over the Water.* Theo Aranson.
*A Companion to Scottish Culture.* David Daiches (Edward Arnold).
*Scotland from the Earliest Times to 1603.* W.C. Dickinson.
*The Normans in Scotland.* R.L.G. Ritchie.
*Scotland: The Making of the Kingdom.* A.A. Duncan.
*Scotland: James V to James VII.* Gordon Donaldson.
*A History of the Scottish People 1560-1830.* T.C. Smout.
*The Jacobite Risings in Britain.* Bruce Lenman.
*Scotland's Forged Tartans: an analytical study of the Vestiarium Scoticum.* D.C. Stewart and J. Charles Thompson (Paul Harris).

# Acknowledgements

I am grateful to the following for their help with the illustration of this book:

Buccleuch Estates, 110; Hamish Brown, 139; Caithness Studios, 184; *The Glasgow Herald*, 18; *The Scotsman*, 82, 190; *The Scottish Field*, 11, 15, 26, 33, 44, 47, 48, 54, 60, 65, 79, 86, 94, 95, 126, 162, 168, 180, 181; The National Galleries of Scotland, 58, 62, 71, 81, 82, 88, 100, 102, 120, 124, 132, 135, 137, 144, 147, 151, 153, 164; The Lord Chamberlain, 90, 112; J. Geddes Wood, *Scotpix*, 185, 192, 194, 196, 198, 200, 202; J. Inglis, 22; David Smith, 13; The Ministry of Public Buildings and Works, 39.

*R.M.*